EURIPIDES IV

HELEN

THE PHOENICIAN WOMEN

ORESTES

THE COMPLETE GREEK TRAGEDIES

Edited by David Grene & Richmond Lattimore

THIRD EDITION *Edited by Mark Griffith & Glenn W. Most*

HELEN *Translated by Richmond Lattimore*

THE PHOENICIAN WOMEN *Translated by Elizabeth Wyckoff*

ORESTES *Translated by William Arrowsmith*

The University of Chicago Press CHICAGO & LONDON

MARK GRIFFITH is professor of classics and of theater, dance, and performance studies at the University of California, Berkeley.

GLENN W. MOST is professor of ancient Greek at the Scuola Normale Superiore at Pisa and a visiting member of the Committee on Social Thought at the University of Chicago.

DAVID GRENE (1913–2002) taught classics for many years at the University of Chicago.

RICHMOND LATTIMORE (1906–1984), professor of Greek at Bryn Mawr College, was a poet and translator best known for his translations of the Greek classics, especially his versions of the *Iliad* and the *Odyssey*.

The University of Chicago Press, Chicago 60637
The University of Chicago Press, Ltd., London
© 2013 by The University of Chicago

Helen © 1956, 2013 by The University of Chicago
Orestes © 1958, 2013 by The University of Chicago
The Phoenician Women © 1959, 2013 by The University of Chicago

22 21 20 19 18 17 16 15 14 13   1 2 3 4 5

ISBN-13: 978-0-226-30895-1 (cloth)
ISBN-13: 978-0-226-30896-8 (paper)
ISBN-13: 978-0-226-30937-8 (e-book)
ISBN-10: 0-226-30895-2 (cloth)
ISBN-10: 0-226-30896-0 (paper)
ISBN-10: 0-226-30937-1 (e-book)

Library of Congress Cataloging-in-Publication Data

Euripides.
  [Works. English. 2012]
  Euripides. — Third edition.
  volumes cm. — (The complete Greek tragedies)
  ISBN 978-0-226-30879-1 (v. 1 : cloth : alk. paper) — ISBN 0-226-30879-0 (v. 1 : cloth : alk. paper) — ISBN 978-0-226-30880-7 (v. 1 : pbk. : alk. paper) — ISBN 0-226-30880-4 (v. 1 : pbk. : alk. paper) — ISBN 978-0-226-30934-7 (v. 1 : e-book) — ISBN 0-226-30934-7 (v. 1 : e-book) — ISBN 978-0-226-30877-7 (v. 2 : cloth : alk. paper) — ISBN 0-226-30877-4 (v. 2 : cloth : alk. paper) — ISBN 978-0-226-30878-4 (v. 2 : pbk. : alk. paper) — ISBN-10: 0-226-30878-2 (v. 2 : pbk. : alk. paper) —ISBN 978-0-226-30935-4 (v. 2 : e-book) —ISBN-10: 0-226-30935-5 (v. 2 : e-book) —ISBN 978-0-226-30881-4 (v. 3 : cloth : alk. paper) — ISBN 0-226-30881-2 (v. 3 : cloth : alk. paper) — ISBN 978-0-226-30882-1 (v. 3 : pbk. : alk. paper) — ISBN 0-226-30882-0 (v. 3 : pbk. : alk. paper) — ISBN 978-0-226-30936-1 (v. 3 : e-book) — ISBN 0-226-30936-3 (v. 3 : e-book)
  1. Euripides—Translations into English. 2. Mythology, Greek—Drama. I. Lattimore, Richmond Alexander, 1906–1984. II. Taplin, Oliver. III. Griffith, Mark, Ph.D. IV. Grene, David. V. Roberts, Deborah H. VI. Arrowsmith, William, 1924–1992. VII. Jones, Frank William Oliver, 1915–. VIII. Vermeule, Emily. IX. Carson, Anne, 1950–. X. Willetts, R. F. (Ronald Frederick), 1915–1999. XI. Euripides. Alcestis. English. XII. Title. XIII. Series: Complete Greek tragedies (Unnumbered)
  PA3975.A1 2012
  882'.01—dc23

                                    2012015831

CONTENTS

EDITORS' PREFACE TO THE THIRD EDITION

The first edition of the *Complete Greek Tragedies*, edited by David Grene and Richmond Lattimore, was published by the University of Chicago Press starting in 1953. But the origins of the series go back even further. David Grene had already published his translation of three of the tragedies with the same press in 1942, and some of the other translations that eventually formed part of the Chicago series had appeared even earlier. A second edition of the series, with new translations of several plays and other changes, was published in 1991. For well over six decades, these translations have proved to be extraordinarily popular and resilient, thanks to their combination of accuracy, poetic immediacy, and clarity of presentation. They have guided hundreds of thousands of teachers, students, and other readers toward a reliable understanding of the surviving masterpieces of the three great Athenian tragedians: Aeschylus, Sophocles, and Euripides.

But the world changes, perhaps never more rapidly than in the past half century, and whatever outlasts the day of its appearance must eventually come to terms with circumstances very different from those that prevailed at its inception. During this same period, scholarly understanding of Greek tragedy has undergone significant development, and there have been marked changes, not only in the readers to whom this series is addressed, but also in the ways in which these texts are taught and studied in universities. These changes have prompted the University of Chicago Press to perform another, more systematic revision of the translations, and we are honored to have been entrusted with this delicate and important task.

Our aim in this third edition has been to preserve and strengthen as far as possible all those features that have made the Chicago translations successful for such a long time, while at the same time revising the texts carefully and tactfully to bring them up to date and equipping them with various kinds of subsidiary help, so they may continue to serve new generations of readers.

Our revisions have addressed the following issues:

- Wherever possible, we have kept the existing translations. But we have revised them where we found this to be necessary in order to bring them closer to the ancient Greek of the original texts or to replace an English idiom that has by now become antiquated or obscure. At the same time, we have done our utmost to respect the original translator's individual style and meter.
- In a few cases, we have decided to substitute entirely new translations for the ones that were published in earlier editions of the series. Euripides' *Medea* has been newly translated by Oliver Taplin, *The Children of Heracles* by Mark Griffith, *Andromache* by Deborah Roberts, and *Iphigenia among the Taurians* by Anne Carson. We have also, in the case of Aeschylus, added translations and brief discussions of the fragments of lost plays that originally belonged to connected tetralogies along with the surviving tragedies, since awareness of these other lost plays is often crucial to the interpretation of the surviving ones. And in the case of Sophocles, we have included a translation of the substantial fragmentary remains of one of his satyr-dramas, *The Trackers* (*Ichneutai*). (See "How the Plays Were Originally Staged" below for explanation of "tetralogy," "satyr-drama," and other terms.)
- We have altered the distribution of the plays among the various volumes in order to reflect the chronological order in which they were written, when this is known or can be estimated with some probability. Thus the *Oresteia* appears now as volume 2 of Aeschylus' tragedies, and the sequence of Euripides' plays has been rearranged.
- We have rewritten the stage directions to make them more consistent throughout, keeping in mind current scholarly under-

standing of how Greek tragedies were staged in the fifth century BCE. In general, we have refrained from extensive stage directions of an interpretive kind, since these are necessarily speculative and modern scholars often disagree greatly about them. The Greek manuscripts themselves contain no stage directions at all.

· We have indicated certain fundamental differences in the meters and modes of delivery of all the verse of these plays. Spoken language (a kind of heightened ordinary speech, usually in the iambic trimeter rhythm) in which the characters of tragedy regularly engage in dialogue and monologue is printed in ordinary Roman font; the sung verse of choral and individual lyric odes (using a large variety of different meters), and the chanted verse recited by the chorus or individual characters (always using the anapestic meter), are rendered in *italics*, with parentheses added where necessary to indicate whether the passage is sung or chanted. In this way, readers will be able to tell at a glance how the playwright intended a given passage to be delivered in the theater, and how these shifting dynamics of poetic register contribute to the overall dramatic effect.

· All the Greek tragedies that survive alternate scenes of action or dialogue, in which individual actors speak all the lines, with formal songs performed by the chorus. Occasionally individual characters sing formal songs too, or they and the chorus may alternate lyrics and spoken verse within the same scene. Most of the formal songs are structured as a series of pairs of stanzas of which the metrical form of the first one ("strophe") is repeated exactly by a second one ("antistrophe"). Thus the metrical structure will be, e.g., strophe A, antistrophe A, strophe B, antistrophe B, with each pair of stanzas consisting of a different sequence of rhythms. Occasionally a short stanza in a different metrical form ("mesode") is inserted in the middle between one strophe and the corresponding antistrophe, and sometimes the end of the whole series is marked with a single stanza in a different metrical form ("epode")—thus, e.g., strophe A, mesode, antistrophe A; or strophe A, antistrophe A, strophe B, antistrophe B, epode. We have indicated these metrical structures by inserting the terms

STROPHE, ANTISTROPHE, MESODE, and EPODE above the first line of the relevant stanzas so that readers can easily recognize the compositional structure of these songs.

- In each play we have indicated by the symbol ° those lines or words for which there are significant uncertainties regarding the transmitted text, and we have explained as simply as possible in textual notes at the end of the volume just what the nature and degree of those uncertainties are. These notes are not at all intended to provide anything like a full scholarly apparatus of textual variants, but instead to make readers aware of places where the text transmitted by the manuscripts may not exactly reflect the poet's own words, or where the interpretation of those words is seriously in doubt.
- For each play we have provided a brief introduction that gives essential information about the first production of the tragedy, the mythical or historical background of its plot, and its reception in antiquity and thereafter.
- For each of the three great tragedians we have provided an introduction to his life and work. It is reproduced at the beginning of each volume containing his tragedies.
- We have also provided at the end of each volume a glossary explaining the names of all persons and geographical features that are mentioned in any of the plays in that volume.

It is our hope that our work will help ensure that these translations continue to delight, to move, to astonish, to disturb, and to instruct many new readers in coming generations.

MARK GRIFFITH, *Berkeley*
GLENN W. MOST, *Florence*

INTRODUCTION TO EURIPIDES

Little is known about the life of Euripides. He was probably born between 485 and 480 BCE on the island of Salamis near Athens. Of the three great writers of Athenian tragedy of the fifth century he was thus the youngest: Aeschylus was older by about forty years, Sophocles by ten or fifteen. Euripides is not reported to have ever engaged significantly in the political or military life of his city, unlike Aeschylus, who fought against the Persians at Marathon, and Sophocles, who was made a general during the Peloponnesian War. In 408 Euripides left Athens to go to the court of King Archelaus of Macedonia in Pella (we do not know exactly why). He died there in 406.

Ancient scholars knew of about ninety plays attributed to Euripides, and he was given permission to participate in the annual tragedy competition at the festival of Dionysus on twenty-two occasions—strong evidence of popular interest in his work. But he was not particularly successful at winning the first prize. Although he began competing in 455 (the year after Aeschylus died), he did not win first place until 441, and during his lifetime he received that award only four times; a fifth victory was bestowed on him posthumously for his trilogy *Iphigenia in Aulis, The Bacchae, Alcmaeon in Corinth* (this last play is lost), produced by one of his sons who was also named Euripides. By contrast, Aeschylus won thirteen victories and Sophocles eighteen. From various references, especially the frequent parodies of Euripides in the comedies of Aristophanes, we can surmise that many members of contemporary Athenian audiences objected to Euripides' tendency to make the characters of tragedy more modern and less heroic, to represent the passions of women, and to reflect recent developments in philosophy and music.

But in the centuries after his death, Euripides went on to become by far the most popular of the Greek tragedians. When the ancient Greeks use the phrase "the poet" without further specification and do not mean by it Homer, they always mean Euripides. Hundreds of fragments from his plays, mostly quite short, are found in quotations by other authors and in anthologies from the period between the third century BCE and the fourth century CE. Many more fragments of his plays have been preserved on papyrus starting in the fourth century BCE than of those by Aeschylus and Sophocles together, and far more scenes of his plays have been associated with images on ancient pottery starting in the same century and on frescoes in Pompeii and elsewhere and Roman sarcophagi some centuries later than is the case for either of his rivals. Some knowledge of his texts spread far and wide through collections of sententious aphorisms and excerpts of speeches and songs drawn from his plays (or invented in his name).

It was above all in the schools that Euripides became the most important author of tragedies: children throughout the Greek-speaking world learned the rules of language and comportment by studying first and foremost Homer and Euripides. But we know that Euripides' plays also continued to be performed in theaters for centuries, and the transmitted texts of some of the more popular ones (e.g., *Medea*, *Orestes*) seem to bear the traces of modifications by ancient producers and actors. Both in his specific plays and plots and in his general conception of dramatic action and character, Euripides massively influenced later Greek playwrights, not only tragic poets but also comic ones (especially Menander, the most important dramatist of New Comedy, born about a century and a half after Euripides)—and not only Greek ones, but Latin ones as well, such as Accius and Pacuvius, and later Seneca (who went on to exert a deep influence on Renaissance drama).

A more or less complete collection of his plays was made in

Alexandria during the third century BCE. Whereas, out of all the plays of Aeschylus and Sophocles, only seven tragedies each were chosen (no one knows by whom) at some point later in antiquity, probably in the second century CE, to represent their work, Euripides received the distinction of having ten plays selected as canonical: *Alcestis, Andromache, The Bacchae, Hecuba, Hippolytus, Medea, Orestes, The Phoenician Women, Rhesus* (scholars generally think this play was written by someone other than Euripides and was attributed to him in antiquity by mistake), and *The Trojan Women*. Of these ten tragedies, three—*Hecuba, Orestes,* and *The Phoenician Women*—were especially popular in the Middle Ages; they are referred to as the Byzantine triad, after the capital of the eastern Empire, Byzantium, known later as Constantinople and today as Istanbul.

The plays that did not form part of the selection gradually ceased to be copied, and thus most of them eventually were lost to posterity. We would possess only these ten plays and fragments of the others were it not for the lucky chance that a single volume of an ancient complete edition of Euripides' plays, arranged alphabetically, managed to survive into the Middle Ages. Thus we also have another nine tragedies (referred to as the alphabetic plays) whose titles in Greek all begin with the letters *epsilon, êta, iota,* and *kappa: Electra, Helen, The Children of Heracles (Hêrakleidai), Heracles, The Suppliant Women (Hiketides), Ion, Iphigenia in Aulis, Iphigenia among the Taurians,* and *The Cyclops (Kyklôps)*. The Byzantine triad have very full ancient commentaries (scholia) and are transmitted by hundreds of medieval manuscripts; the other seven plays of the canonical selection have much sparser scholia and are transmitted by something more than a dozen manuscripts; the alphabetic plays have no scholia at all and are transmitted only by a single manuscript in rather poor condition and by its copies.

Modern scholars have been able to establish a fairly secure dating for most of Euripides' tragedies thanks to the exact indications provided by ancient scholarship for the first production of some of them and the relative chronology suggested by metrical and other features for the others. Accordingly the five volumes of this third edition have been organized according to the probable chronological sequence:

Volume 1:   *Alcestis*: 438 BCE
             Medea: 431
             The Children of Heracles: ca. 430
             Hippolytus: 428
Volume 2:   *Andromache*: ca. 425
             Hecuba: ca. 424
             The Suppliant Women: ca. 423
             Electra: ca. 420
Volume 3:   *Heracles*: ca. 415
             The Trojan Women: 415
             Iphigenia among the Taurians: ca. 414
             Ion: ca. 413
Volume 4:   *Helen*: 412
             The Phoenician Women: ca. 409
             Orestes: 408
Volume 5:   *The Bacchae*: posthumously after 406
             Iphigenia in Aulis: posthumously after 406
             The Cyclops: date unknown
             Rhesus: probably spurious, from the fourth century BCE

In the Renaissance Euripides remained the most popular of the three tragedians. Directly and by the mediation of Seneca he influenced drama from the sixteenth to the eighteenth century far more than Aeschylus or Sophocles did. But toward the end of the eighteenth century and even more in the course of the nineteenth century, he came increasingly under attack yet again, as already in the fifth century BCE, and for much the same reason, as being decadent, tawdry, irreligious, and inharmonious. He was also criticized for his perceived departures from the ideal of "the tragic" (as exemplified by plays such as Sophocles' *Oedipus the*

King and *Antigone*), especially in the "romance" plots of *Alcestis, Iphigenia among the Taurians, Ion,* and *Helen.* It was left to the twentieth century to discover its own somewhat disturbing affinity to his tragic style and worldview. Nowadays among theatrical audiences, scholars, and nonprofessional readers Euripides is once again at least as popular as his two rivals.

HOW THE PLAYS WERE ORIGINALLY STAGED

Nearly all the plays composed by Aeschylus, Sophocles, and Euripides were first performed in the Theater of Dionysus at Athens, as part of the annual festival and competition in drama. This was not only a literary and musical event, but also an important religious and political ceremony for the Athenian community. Each year three tragedians were selected to compete, with each of them presenting four plays per day, a "tetralogy" of three tragedies and one satyr-play. The satyr-play was a type of drama similar to tragedy in being based on heroic myth and employing many of the same stylistic features, but distinguished by having a chorus of half-human, half-horse followers of Dionysus—sileni or satyrs—and by always ending happily. Extant examples of this genre are Euripides' *The Cyclops* (in *Euripides*, vol. 5) and Sophocles' *The Trackers* (partially preserved: in *Sophocles*, vol. 2).

The three competing tragedians were ranked by a panel of citizens functioning as amateur judges, and the winner received an honorific prize. Records of these competitions were maintained, allowing Aristotle and others later to compile lists of the dates when each of Aeschylus', Sophocles', and Euripides' plays were first performed and whether they placed first, second, or third in the competition (unfortunately we no longer possess the complete lists).

The tragedians competed on equal terms: each had at his disposal three actors (only two in Aeschylus' and Euripides' earliest plays) who would often have to switch between roles as each play progressed, plus other nonspeaking actors to play attendants and other subsidiary characters; a chorus of twelve (in Aeschylus' time) or fifteen (for most of the careers of Sophocles and Euripides), who would sing and dance formal songs and whose Chorus Leader would engage in dialogue with the characters or offer comment on the action; and a pipe-player, to accompany the sung portions of the play.

All the performers were men, and the actors and chorus members all wore masks. The association of masks with other Dionysian rituals may have affected their use in the theater; but masks had certain practical advantages as well—for example, making it easy to play female characters and to change quickly between roles. In general, the use of masks also meant that ancient acting techniques must have been rather different from what we are used to seeing in the modern theater. Acting in a mask requires a more frontal and presentational style of performance toward the audience than is usual with unmasked, "realistic" acting; a masked actor must communicate far more by voice and stylized bodily gesture than by facial expression, and the gradual development of a character in the course of a play could hardly be indicated by changes in his or her mask. Unfortunately, however, we know almost nothing about the acting techniques of the Athenian theater. But we do know that the chorus members were all Athenian amateurs, and so were the actors up until the later part of the fifth century, by which point a prize for the best actor had been instituted in the tragic competition, and the art of acting (which of course included solo singing and dancing) was becoming increasingly professionalized.

The tragedian himself not only wrote the words for his play but also composed the music and choreography and directed the productions. It was said that Aeschylus also acted in his plays but that Sophocles chose not to, except early in his career, because his voice was too weak. Euripides is reported to have had a collaborator who specialized in musical composition. The costs for each playwright's production were shared between an individual wealthy citizen, as a kind of "super-tax" requirement, and the city.

The Theater of Dionysus itself during most of the fifth century BCE probably consisted of a large rectangular or trapezoidal dance floor, backed by a one-story wooden building (the *skênê*), with a large central door that opened onto the dance floor. (Some scholars have argued that two doors were used, but the evidence is thin.) Between the *skênê* and the dance floor there may have been a narrow stage on which the characters acted and which communicated easily with the dance floor. For any particular play, the *skênê* might represent a palace, a house, a temple, or a cave, for example; the interior of this "building" was generally invisible to the audience, with all the action staged in front of it. Sophocles is said to have been the first to use painted scenery; this must have been fairly simple and easy to remove, as every play had a different setting. Playwrights did not include stage directions in their texts. Instead, a play's setting was indicated explicitly by the speaking characters.

All the plays were performed in the open air and in daylight. Spectators sat on wooden seats in rows, probably arranged in rectangular blocks along the curving slope of the Acropolis. (The stone semicircular remains of the Theater of Dionysus that are visible today in Athens belong to a later era.) Seating capacity seems to have been four to six thousand—thus a mass audience, but not quite on the scale of the theaters that came to be built during the fourth century BCE and later at Epidaurus, Ephesus, and many other locations all over the Mediterranean.

Alongside the *skênê*, on each side, there were passages through which actors could enter and exit. The acting area included the dance floor, the doorway, and the area immediately in front of the *skênê*. Occasionally an actor appeared on the roof or above it, as if flying. He was actually hanging from a crane (*mêchanê*: hence *deus ex machina*, "a god from the machine"). The *skênê* was also occasionally opened up—the mechanical details are uncertain—in order to show the audience what was concealed within (usually dead bodies). Announcements of entrances and exits, like the setting, were made by the characters. Although the medieval manuscripts of the surviving plays do not provide explicit stage directions, it is usually possible to infer from the words or from the context whether a particular entrance or exit is being made through a door (into the *skênê*) or by one of the side entrances. In later antiquity, there may have been a rule that one side entrance always led to the city center, the other to the countryside or harbor. Whether such a rule was ever observed in the fifth century is uncertain.

HELEN

Translated by RICHMOND LATTIMORE

HELEN: INTRODUCTION

The Play: Date and Composition

We know from external evidence that Euripides' *Helen* was first produced in 412 BCE. Presumably Euripides wrote it for the annual competition at the Great Dionysian Festival in Athens. One of the other tragedies staged together with it was *Andromeda*, which is known only from fragments and later references; what the other two plays were in Euripides' tetralogy of that year, and how they fared in the dramatic competition, are unknown.

The Myth

How was it possible that for the sake of one woman, Helen, a whole Greek army could wage war against Troy for ten long years and at the end completely destroy the city? And how could Helen's notorious marital infidelity (she abandoned her husband Menelaus and her daughter Hermione to elope with the Trojan prince Paris) be reconciled with the fact that she was worshipped as a goddess in Sparta? Already within the *Iliad* and *Odyssey* Homer, our earliest source, hints at some perplexity about these questions, and, while retaining the terms of the traditional story, he pointedly allows Helen's reputation and the degree to which she is to be blamed for the war to remain disputed and unresolved.

Some later authors felt freer to change the story itself. About a century before Euripides, the lyric poet Stesichorus claimed that Helen had blinded him for telling the traditional version and that his sight had been restored when he went on to compose a "Palinode" that asserted, "This story is not true, / You did not go in the well-benched ships / And you did not arrive at the towers of Troy." Stesichorus' famous lyric poem apparently said that it was a phantom likeness of Helen that went with Paris to Troy in her stead while she herself stayed in Egypt under the protection of King Proteus; but this poem has been almost completely lost, and we can only guess at its details. A couple of decades before Euripides' *Helen*, the historian Herodotus told his own version: Paris abducted Helen from Sparta, but on their way back to Troy they were blown off course to Egypt; when the Egyptian king Proteus found out what Paris was up to, he kept Helen safe with him and sent Paris back to Troy without her: for ten years the Greeks fought the Trojans under the mistaken belief that Helen was in Troy (when the Trojans told them the truth, the Greeks did not believe them); the Greeks found out when they won the war and sacked the city, and afterward Menelaus, sailing back to Greece, stopped in Egypt, picked Helen up, and took her home.

Euripides' *Helen* develops further Stesichorus' two crucial innovations, Helen's phantom likeness and her stay in Egypt. According to Euripides' version, Hera, furious that Aphrodite won the Judgment of Paris by promising him Helen, has substituted for her a phantom likeness over which the Greeks and Trojans have combated at Troy for ten years under the mistaken impression that it was the real thing. In the meantime the real Helen has been kept safe by the virtuous Proteus in Egypt. Now the Trojan War is over, and Menelaus, returning home with the phantom Helen, is shipwrecked off the coast of Egypt—where Proteus has died and his unvirtuous son Theoclymenus is trying to marry Helen and threatens to kill any Greek he finds. The play begins with Helen as a suppliant at Proteus' tomb desperately seeking protection against Theoclymenus' advances. Menelaus arrives at the palace, dressed in rags, and after considerable confusion husband and wife joyously recognize one another (meanwhile the phantom Helen has flown back to heaven). Helen devises a clever stratagem to allow the Greeks to escape from Theoclymenus' clutches, with the help of his prophetic sister Theonoë. At the end Helen's divine brothers Castor and Polydeuces manifest themselves to calm the angry Theoclymenus and to predict the future.

Helen of Troy is almost always an extremely negative character in Greek tragedy, which generally presupposes the Homeric version of events. The story Euripides dramatizes in this play seems not to have featured in any earlier tragedy, though it is possible that Aeschylus included a version of it in his *Proteus*, the satyr-play that was produced fourth in the *Oresteia* tetralogy. Euripides' *Helen* does bear obvious similarities to his *Iphigenia among the Taurians*, which he probably staged a couple of years earlier. In both plays, a virtuous Greek woman is held captive among barbarians, is surprisingly reunited with a beloved male family member, and by devising an ingenious plan manages to escape by sea and return home with him; she outwits her barbarian captor and at the end a *deus ex machina* appears so as to put matters in order. But whereas *Iphigenia* tended to focus more on an exciting plot, the mechanics of the recognition, and the psychology of its main characters, *Helen* raises intriguing questions concerning morality, religion, and cultural difference. In particular, it uses the bizarre situation of Helen's phantom likeness in order to explore general problems of human knowledge that had been posed by recent philosophers and sophists like Gorgias and Protagoras. Can we really believe what we see or be sure that we know what we think we know? Can we trust our senses? If not, what guarantees of truth or reality, divine or human, do exist in the world? These are problems with which contemporary intellectuals were wrestling; and Euripides' version of the story of Helen provides a witty and ingenious test case in order to scrutinize them. *Helen* also presents an example of happy and successful conjugal love, rare in Greek tragedy. Helen's fidelity, the restitution of her good name, and Menelaus' joyous reunion with her are central themes in the play.

Transmission and Reception

Helen seems to have had a considerable impact when it was first produced, at least to judge by the extensive (and hilarious) parody of the play in Aristophanes' *Women at the Thesmophoria*, produced the very next year, in 411 BCE. But thereafter the traces of its influence on ancient literature are very few indeed—perhaps some allusions by the New Comedy playwright Menander, and certainly the fourth-century BCE Alexandrian poet Lycophron's enigmatic *Alexandra*, a dramatic lyric about Cassandra and the Trojan War. And it does not seem to have influenced ancient art at all—by contrast, *Andromeda*, another of the tragedies that was produced by Euripides together with *Helen* at the same year's dramatic festival and that also dealt with exotic adventures and requited love, made a considerable impact on subsequent Greek and Roman visual culture. In general it was Homer's canonical version of Helen that dominated in antiquity over Stesichorus', Herodotus', and Euripides' eccentric ones. *Helen* survived antiquity as one of the so-called "alphabetic plays" (see "Introduction to Euripides," p. 3) in only a single manuscript (and its copies), and it is not accompanied by the ancient commentaries (scholia) that explain various kinds of interpretive difficulties. But evidence that it achieved at least a small degree of popularity in antiquity is provided by the fact that at least one papyrus bearing parts of its text has been discovered.

In the modern world too, *Helen* has not been as popular as it deserves to be: the dominance of Homer's canonical version, together with Euripides' disconcerting and sometimes comic representation of divine manipulation of human affairs, seems until recently to have discouraged both readers and stage producers. But all of the few authors who have engaged with Euripides' play have produced remarkably interesting versions of the story. In his *Sonnets pour Hélène* (1578), Pierre de Ronsard exploits both versions of Helen in order to work through his contradictory feelings for his beloved, Hélène de Surgères. Jacques Offenbach's comic opera *La Belle Hélène* (1864) followed the Homeric story line; but Richard Strauss' extraordinary opera *Die ägyptische Helena* (*The Egyptian Helen*, 1928), from a libretto by Hugo von Hofmannsthal, adapts and reverses crucial aspects of Euripides' plot (here the Homeric version is the true one, but the Egyptian tale is invented in order to persuade Menelaus to take Helen back) in order to explore, with complex music and profound psychology, the fundamental themes of love, trust, and memory. In contrast, George Seferis' brief lyric poem "Helen" (1953) uses the Euripidean story to point out the futile butchery involved in all wars; and *Helen in Egypt* (1961), a lengthy prose poem by H.D. (Hilda Doolittle), criticizes war, epic, and traditional male values from a feminist standpoint. In modern times the play has been produced relatively rarely except on college campuses and at Greek festivals. But recent years have seen a growing interest in it, and an adaptation by Frank McGuinness, directed by Deborah Bruce, had a successful run in London (2009).

HELEN

Characters   HELEN, wife of Menelaus
TEUCER, Greek chieftain, brother of Ajax
CHORUS of Greek captive women
MENELAUS, husband of Helen
DOORKEEPER, an old woman, slave of
Theoclymenus
SERVANT of Menelaus
THEONOË, sister of Theoclymenus
THEOCLYMENUS, king of Egypt
MESSENGER, servant of Theoclymenus
SERVANT of Theonoë
CASTOR, divine brother of Helen
POLYDEUCES, twin brother of Castor
(nonspeaking)

*Scene: The palace of Theoclymenus in Egypt. In front is the tomb of
King Proteus, the father of Theoclymenus. Helen is discovered sitting
against the tomb as a suppliant.*

HELEN

These are the waters of the Nile, stream of sweet nymphs.
The river, fed with melting of pale snows, and not
with rain, rises to flood the flats of Egypt. Here
Proteus, while yet he lived, was lord over the land,
at home in Pharos, king in Egypt;° and his bride   5
was Psamathe, one of the daughters of the deep,
wife once to Aeacus, later sundered from him,

who bore two children to him in the house, a boy
called Theoclymenus (because his father showed
the gods love in his lifetime)° and a fine girl they named   10
Eido, her mother's glory when she was a child;
but when she came to nubile age they changed her name
to Theonoë, for she understood the gods' concerns,
all things that are and will be, by means of divination.
Nereus, her forefather, granted her this privilege.   15

Nor is my own country obscure. It is a place
called Sparta, and my father was Tyndareus: though
they tell a story about how Zeus took on himself
the shape of a flying swan, with eagle in pursuit,
and came on wings to Leda my mother, and so won   20
the act of love by treachery. Or so they say.
They called me Helen. Let me tell you all the evils,
all that has happened to me. The three goddesses came
to remote Ida, and to Paris, for him to judge
their loveliness, and beauty was the cause. These were   25
Hera, Cypris, and Zeus' daughter Athena.
But Aphrodite, promising my loveliness
(if what is cursed is ever lovely) to the arms
of Paris, won her way. Idaean Paris left
his herds for Sparta, thinking I was to be his.   30
But Hera, angry that she was not given the prize,
made void as wind the love that might have been for Paris
and gave him, not me, but in my likeness fashioning
a breathing image out of the sky's air, bestowed
this on King Priam's son, who thinks he holds me now   35
but holds a vanity which is not I. See, next,
how further counsels of Zeus add to my misery.
He loaded war upon the Hellenic land and on
the unhappy Phrygians, thus to ease our mother earth
of the burden and the multitude of humankind,   40
and also to advertise the greatest Hellene prince.
The Phrygians fought for me (except it was not I

but my name only) held against the spears of Greece.
I myself was caught up by Hermes into the sky,
hidden in a cloud, for Zeus had not forgotten me,   45
and set down by him where you see me, in the house
of Proteus, chosen because, most temperate of men,
he could guard my honor safe for Menelaus. So
here am I; but meanwhile my ill-adventured lord
assembled an armament to track me down the trail   50
of my abduction, and assaulted Ilium's towers.
Because of me, beside the waters of Scamander, lives
were lost in numbers; and I who've endured so much—
I'm cursed by all and thought to have betrayed my lord
and for the Hellenes lit the flame of a great war.   55

Why do I go on living, then? Yet I have heard
from the god Hermes that I yet shall remake my home
in the famous plain of Sparta with my lord, and he
shall know I never went to Ilium—if I've not shared
my bed with any other man. While Proteus still looked   60
upon this sun we see, I was safe from marriage. Now
that he is dead and hidden in the dark, his son
pursues me for my hand, but I, remembering
my first husband, cling a suppliant here upon
the grave of Proteus, for help to keep my marriage safe.   65
Thus, though I wear the name of guilt in Greece, yet here
I'll keep my body uncontaminated by disgrace.

(Enter Teucer from the side.)

TEUCER
What master holds dominion in these lowering halls?
The scope of wall is royal, and the massive pile
bespeaks possession by the Lord of Gold and Death.   70

(Seeing Helen.)

Ah!
O gods, what do I see before me. Do I see
the deadly likeness of that woman who destroyed

all the Achaeans and me? May the gods spurn you for
looking so much like Helen's copy. Were I not   75
footfast on alien ground, with my true-winging shaft
I would have killed you, for looking like the child of Zeus.

HELEN

Poor wretch, whoever you are, whatever cause has driven
you here, why must her sorrows turn your hate on *me*?

TEUCER

I was wrong so to give way to anger more   80
than it became me. All Greece hates the child of Zeus.
Therefore forgive me, lady, for what I have said.

HELEN

But who are you? From what country have you journeyed
here?

TEUCER

Lady, I am one of those unfortunate Greeks.

HELEN

It is no wonder you hate Helen then. But tell°   85
me who you are. Where from? Whose son should you be
called?

TEUCER

My name is Teucer, and the father who gave me life
is Telamon. The land of Salamis nursed my youth.

HELEN

And what has brought you to this valley of the Nile?

TEUCER

I am an exile, driven from my father's land.   90

HELEN

You must be unhappy. Who was it who forced you out?

TEUCER

Telamon, my father. Who should be nearer to my love?

HELEN

But why? Such action means catastrophe for you.

TEUCER

Ajax my brother died at Troy. This meant my doom.

HELEN

Surely it was not by your sword he lost his life?   95

TEUCER

His death came when he hurled himself on his own blade.

HELEN

In frenzy? Could a sane man see such an act through?

TEUCER

You have heard of one they call Achilles, Peleus' son.

HELEN

Yes.
He came once to ask for Helen's hand; so we are told.

TEUCER

He was killed. His armor caused a quarrel among his friends.   100

HELEN

But how could all this have brought Ajax any harm?   .

TEUCER

Someone else won the armor, and he killed himself.

HELEN

But has this suffering of his damaged your life?

TEUCER

Yes, if only because I did not die with him.

HELEN

I see. Tell me, were you at famous Ilium, then?   105

TEUCER

I helped sack it. That act has been my own ruin.

HELEN

And the city has been set afire? It is all gone?

TEUCER

You could no longer tell for sure where the walls stood.

HELEN

Helen, poor wretch! The Phrygians have perished for your
sake.

TEUCER

The Achaeans also; for great evil has been done.   110

HELEN

How long is it now since the city was destroyed?

TEUCER

Seven years have almost circled with their crops since then.

HELEN

How much time in addition did you spend at Troy?

TEUCER

Moon after moon, until it came to ten full years.

HELEN

And then you got the woman of Sparta?

TEUCER

Yes we did.   115
Menelaus seized her by the hair and dragged her off.

HELEN

Did you see the poor woman, or have you only heard?

TEUCER

I saw her with my own eyes, as I see you now.

HELEN

Think. Could this be only an impression, caused by god?

TEUCER

Speak of some other matter, please. No more of her.   120

HELEN

You do believe your impression is infallible.°

TEUCER

These eyes saw her. When the eyes see, the mind sees too.

HELEN

So. Then by now Menelaus and his wife are home.

TEUCER

They are not in Argos, nor where the Eurotas runs.

HELEN

You speak them ill, and, ah, you tell of ills for them.   125

TEUCER

The rumor is that he has vanished with his wife.

HELEN

Then all the Argives did not sail for home together?

TEUCER

They did, but a storm split them and drove them variously.

HELEN

Among what waves, where on the open sea?

TEUCER

                                                        Just as
they cut across the middle of the Aegean main.   130

HELEN

And after this, none knows of Menelaus' return?

TEUCER

No one does; and in Greece he is reported dead.

HELEN

Then I am undone.
                           Is Thestius' daughter still alive?

TEUCER

You mean by this Leda? No, she is dead and gone.

HELEN

It could not have been the shame of Helen that caused her
  death?   135

TEUCER

They say so; that she fastened the noose on her fair throat.

HELEN

Tyndareus' sons, then; are they alive, or are they not?

TEUCER

Dead, not dead. There are two interpretations here.

HELEN

Which one prevails? How much sorrow must I endure?

TEUCER

Men say that they have been made stars and are divine.   140

HELEN

Fair told when thus told; but what is the other account?

TEUCER

That for their sister's shame they died by their own hands.
Enough words now. I should not have to suffer twice.
But for the matter of my errand to this house
of kings, it was my wish to see Theonoë   145
the prophetess. Be you my representative
and help me learn from her how I should steer the wings
of my ship with best wind for the sea-girt land
of Cyprus, where Apollo prophesied that I
should found and name New Salamis from my island home. 150

HELEN

Sail, friend. Your course will show itself; but you must leave
this country and escape before you have been seen
by the son of Proteus, ruler of this land. He now
has gone with hounds, hopeful of killing beasts of chase.
He slaughters every Greek he lays his hands upon,   155

but why he does this, you must not try to find out,
as I am silent. For how could my speech help you?

TEUCER

All you have said was good, my lady, and may the gods
grant you the grace your kindness has deserved. You wear
the bodily shape of Helen, but you have a heart   160
that is not hers. Wide is the difference. May she
die miserably, never see Eurotas' stream
again.

    But may you, lady, always prosper well.

(Exit to the side.)

HELEN [*singing*]

Here, beginning a song of deep wretchedness for the depth of my
    sorrows,
what shall be the strain of my threnody, what singing spirit   165
supplicate in tears, in mourning, in sorrow? Oh, oh!

STROPHE A

You who go winged women in form
young and maiden, daughters of Earth,
O Sirens, if you would only come°   170
to attend my mourning
with Libyan reed, with Pan-pipes,
with lyres, with tears of your own to give
the singing of all my unhappiness.
With sufferings for sufferings, sorrows for sorrows,
melody matching
my dirges, given
by Persephone   175
of the dead,° she in turn shall be given
in her halls of night the sweet of my sorrow
in consecration
of those who are dead and gone from us.

(Enter the Chorus from the side.)

CHORUS [*singing in this lyric interchange with Helen, who sings in reply*]

ANTISTROPHE A

I was down by the shining blue
water, and on the curl of the grass   180
there in the golden glare of the sun°
laid out the colored laundry
in the bed of the young rushes
to dry. There I heard my lady
and the pitiful sound as she cried out,
the voice of sorrow,° lament without lyres,   185
a sharp voice of pain, of mourning
as cries aloud for grief some nymph,
a Naiad, caught
in the hills for all her flight,° gives voice
to pain, as under the rock hollows
she cries out
on Pan and his violent union with her.   190

HELEN

STROPHE B

Hear me,
spoil of the barbarian oar blade,
daughters of Greece, hear:
from Achaea a mariner
came, yes came, and tears on my tears he loaded.   195
The wrecked city of Ilium
is given up to the teeth of fire,
all through me and the deaths I caused,
all for my name of affliction. So
Leda has taken her life within   200
the strangling noose, for the thought of shame
in those sorrows that has been mine.
My lord is lost, he is gone, far driven
over the sea. And the twin-born glory
of the land of my father, Castor   205
and Polydeuces his brother, vanished,

vanished away; the plain where their horses
trampled, their wrestling ground, desolate
down by the reeds of Eurotas   210
where the young men rode and trained.

CHORUS

Ah me,
so sorrowful was that destiny,
lady mine, that befell you,
a life better unlived
given to you, yes given, when Zeus blazed in the bright
air, in the snowflash of the swan's   215
wing to beget you upon your mother.
What grief is there you have not known?
What in life have you not lived through?
Your mother is lost and gone;
the twins, beloved children of Zeus,   220
are blessed in fortune no longer. Your eyes
are kept from the sight of your country,
while through the cities of men there goes
the rumor, divine lady, that gives
you up to barbarian lusts. And now   225
your husband, lost on the tossing sea,
is gone from life. He will come no more
to bless the halls of his father, bless
the brazen house of Athena.

HELEN

What man of the Phrygians was it
or was it one from Hellenic soil   230
who cut down the dripping pine timbers
fatal to Ilium?
This was the timber that Priam's son
shaped into that accursed ship
which, driven by barbarian oars, brought him

to the hearth where I lived; he came°   235
for my ill-starred beauty,
to capture my love.
And she, the treacherous goddess,
the murderous queen of Cyprus,
drew death down on the Danaid men,°
cruel in all her working.   240
Then Hera, goddess of grandeur,
queen of the golden throne, who lies
in the arms of Zeus, sent down to me
Hermes, fleet son of Maia.
I was picking fresh flowers,
gathering them into my robe, to take
to Athena there in her brazen house   245
when he caught me away through the bright
air to this unprofitable
country, poor me, made a prize of war
for Priam's sons and the Hellenes;
while upon my name
where Simois runs has descended   250
a false fame and a vanity.

CHORUS LEADER

You have your sorrows, I know it well. But it were best
to bear your life's constraints as lightly as you may.

HELEN [*now speaking*]

Women and friends, what is this destiny on which   255
I am fastened? Was I born a monster among mankind?
No woman, neither in Greece nor yet in Barbary,°
is hatched from the white envelope that contains young birds,
yet thus Leda bore me to Zeus, or so they say.
And so my life is monstrous, and so are the things that
    happen   260
to me, through Hera, or my beauty is to blame.
I wish that like a picture I had been rubbed out
and done again, made plain, without this loveliness,

for so the Greeks would never have been aware of all
those misfortunes that now are mine. So I would keep   265
what was not bad, as now they keep the bad of me.
He who sees from the gods a single strain of luck,
all bad, has a sad lot, but can endure it still.
More complex is the sorrow in which I am involved.
I have done nothing wrong and yet my reputation   270
is bad, and worse than a true evil is it to bear
the burden of faults that aren't truly one's own. Again,
the gods have torn me from my father's land and made
me live among barbarians. I have no kin
here and I live a slave although my birth was free.   275
All Barbary is slave except a single man.
There was one anchor to my hope: the thought of how
my husband might come some day and deliver me,
but gone is that hope now, for he is dead and gone.
My mother is dead—I am her murderer. I know   280
that is unfair, but such unfairness I must accept.
My daughter, pride of the household and my own pride,
is growing to gray years unmarried. And the sons
of Zeus, or so men call them, the Dioscuri,
no longer live. So all my luck is turned to grief   285
and for all purposes I'm dead, though I live in fact.
But worst of all is, if I ever should win home°
the gates would shut me out, for all men think that I
am that Helen whom Menelaus went to Troy
to get. If my husband were alive, I could be known   290
by him through signs which no one else could know about.
But this fails now. It cannot be that he lives still.
Why do I go on living then? What fate is left?
Shall I choose marriage as my means to get away
from hardship? Live with a barbarian husband? Sit   295
at a rich table? No, for when a woman hates
the husband she lives with, she hates her body too.
Death is best. But to die in some unseemly way?°
When one hangs by the neck, it is ugly

and is thought a bad sight even when slaves die so.　　　　300
Death by the knife is noble and has dignity,
but it's hard to find the mortal spot to end one's life.
Such is the depth of my unhappiness, that while
for other women beauty means their happiness
it is my very beauty that has ruined me.　　　　305

CHORUS LEADER
Helen, you should not be so sure that that stranger
who came, whoever he is, has spoken all the truth.

HELEN
But he said plainly that my husband had been lost.

CHORUS LEADER
Many things are said plainly, yet prove to be false.

HELEN
Yes, but on the other side, they may be true.　　　　310

CHORUS LEADER
You push yourself to believe the worst and not the best.

HELEN
Yes, I am frightened, and so led by fright to terror.

CHORUS LEADER
How does your favor stand with those inside the house?

HELEN
All here are friends, except the man who hunts my love.

CHORUS LEADER
Do you know? I think you should leave your place at the
tomb . . .　　　　315

HELEN
What advice is it you so hesitantly give?

CHORUS LEADER
Go to the house, and ask the daughter of the sea's

nymph, ask Theonoë, who understands all things,
about your husband, whether he still lives, or if
he is lost from daylight. Then, when you are well informed,   320
be happy, or be sorry, as your luck deserves.
Now, when you really know nothing, where is the use
in hurting yourself as you do now? Do what I say.
Give up the shelter of this tomb. Speak with the girl.°
Why look further, when in this very house you have   325
a source of knowledge that will tell you all the truth?
I volunteer to go inside the house with you
and help you ask the maiden for her prophecies.
It is right for women to stand by a woman's cause.

HELEN [*singing in this lyric interchange with the Chorus, who sing in
reply*]

Friends, I accept your argument.   330
Go, then, go inside the house
so that there you may ask
what new trials await me now.

CHORUS

I will, nor hesitate. Urge not.

HELEN

O pitiful day.   335
Unhappy I, unhappy, oh what
tale of tears shall I be told?

CHORUS

Do not be prophetic of grief.
Do not, dear, anticipate sorrow.

HELEN

My poor husband, what has happened to him?   340
Do his eyes see the light,
the Sun's chariot and four horses, the stars in course,
or among dead men under ground
is his fate long-lasting?   345

CHORUS
   Whatever the future
   will bring, consider best.

HELEN
   I call upon you by name, I invoke,
   river pale by the washed reeds,
   Eurotas; if this tale   350
   of my lord's death that has come to me
   is true—and where was the story not clear?—°
   then I will bind my throat
   fast in the hanging noose of death,
   or with the deadly stroke that cuts
   the throat open and bleeding   355
   drive the iron with my own hand hard into my body,
   a sacrifice to the trinity
   of goddesses, and to Priam's son
   who held the hollows of Ida
   long ago when he tended his herds.

CHORUS
   From somewhere may defense emerge   360
   against evils: may your fortune turn.

HELEN
   Ah, Troy, the unhappy,
   for things done that were never done
   you died, hurt pitifully. The gifts
   the Lady of Cyprus gave me brought
   showers of tears, showers of blood, pain°   365
   on pain, tears upon tears, suffering.
   Mothers who saw their children die,
   maidens who cut their long hair
   for kinsmen who were killed beside the waters
   of Phrygian Scamander.
   Hellas too has cried, has cried   370
   aloud in lamentation,
   beaten her hands against her head

and with the nails' track of blood
torn her cheeks' softness.

Blessed long ago in Arcadia, maiden Callisto,   375
you who shared the bed of Zeus and then were made
into a four-foot beast, how happy was your lot beside
my own; for all the bear's shaggy bulk
is made gentle by the soft eyes,°
and the metamorphosis took away   380
your sorrows. Artemis drove from her dances
the doe of the golden horns, Titanian daughter of Merops,
for her loveliness. But my body's beauty
ruined the citadel of the Dardanians, ruined
all the perished Achaeans.   385

(Exit all into the palace. Enter Menelaus from
the side, dressed in tattered clothing.)

MENELAUS
Ah Pelops, racer of chariots and horses long
ago with Oenomaus in the Pisan field,
how I could wish that, when you were constrained to make°
an offering to the gods, you had then left this life
for theirs, before you had sired my father, Atreus;   390
who by his marriage with Aerope begot
Agamemnon and myself, Menelaus, two renowned
brothers; for here I do not boast, yet I believe
we marshalled the greatest of armadas against Troy
although we led them not as tyrants, not by force,   395
but the young men of Greece willingly served with us.
Those who are no more living can be numbered now,
and those who, gratefully escaping from the sea,
brought home again the names of all the dead. But I,
battered and driven over the gray swell of the open   400
sea, have been wandering ever since I stormed the towers
of Ilium, trying to get back to my own land
whereto the gods debar my right of homecoming.

I have now sailed to all the friendless, desolate
approaches of Libya; always, as I make near home,   405
the wind buffets me back again, nor ever fills
favorably my sail to bring me home again.

     And now, hapless and shipwrecked, with my friends all lost,
I am driven upon this shore. My ship shattered against
the rocks, and broke up into wreck and flotsam there.   410
Of all the ship's various parts only the keel held out,
and on it, by some unexpected chance, I managed
to save myself and Helen, whom I seized from Troy.
What this land is I do not know, nor yet the name
of its people; I was too embarrassed to be seen   415
in public, could not ask,° but tried to hide away
my ragged state in shame for my bad luck. For when
a great man falls upon evil chance, the strangeness of it
makes him feel worse than the man accustomed to hard times.
But the need is too much for me, for we have no food   420
nor any clothing for our skin, as you may guess
by the kind of ship's flotsam in which I wrap myself.
The robes and all the shining wraps I had before
are lost at sea with all my treasures. Deep inside
a cave I hid the wife who was the cause of all   425
my evil fortunes, and constrained those friends who still
are left alive to keep her safe for me. So now
I am here, all by myself, to see if I can raise
some provisions to take to the friends I left behind.
I saw this house with its expanse of masonry   430
and the grand gates as of some fortunate man, and so
came here. Seafarers always hope for charity
from the houses of the rich. Those who themselves are poor
would not be able to help us, though the wish were there.
O-ay! Who is the porter here? Will he come out   435
and take the message of my griefs to those inside?

     (*Enter Theoclymenus' Doorkeeper, an old woman, from the palace.*)

DOORKEEPER

    Who is at the gates? Go away, will you, from the house?
    Do not keep standing here before the courtyard doors
    and bothering the masters. It will mean your death.
    You are a Greek, and Greeks are not allowed in here.   440

MENELAUS

    Quite so, granny, just as you say, and fair enough.°
    Very well, I will do what you say, only let me talk.

DOORKEEPER

    Out with you. I have orders, stranger, never to let
    anyone who comes from Greece approach near to this house.

MENELAUS

    Ah! Keep your hands off me, and stop pushing me.   445

DOORKEEPER

    That is your fault. You are not doing what I say.

MENELAUS

    Now go inside and take this message to your master . . .

DOORKEEPER

    There'll be suffering ahead if I take a message from you.°

MENELAUS

    I am a shipwrecked guest and so I am protected.

DOORKEEPER

    Go on then to some other house instead of this.   450

MENELAUS

    No, I am going in; do as I tell you to.

DOORKEEPER

    I tell you, you are bothersome. We'll throw you out.

MENELAUS

    Ah, where are all my armies now, which won such fame?

DOORKEEPER

You may have been a great man at home. You are not one here.

MENELAUS

God, what a loss of station, and how undeserved! 455

DOORKEEPER

Your eyes are wet with tears. Tell me, why are you sad?

MENELAUS

Thinking of all my happiness in times gone by.

DOORKEEPER

Go then, bestow those tears upon your own people.

MENELAUS

Tell me first, what is this country, what king's house is this?

DOORKEEPER

This is the house of Proteus; Egypt is the land. 460

MENELAUS

Egypt? What an unhappy chance to have sailed here!

DOORKEEPER

What do you find wrong with the glories of the Nile?

MENELAUS

Nothing wrong. It is my own bad luck that makes me sad.

DOORKEEPER

There are many men who have bad luck, not only you.

MENELAUS

Is there some ruler in the house you could name to me? 465

DOORKEEPER

This is his tomb you see here. Now his son is king.

MENELAUS

Where would he be then? In the house, or gone somewhere?

DOORKEEPER

He is not in; and above all else he hates Hellenes.

MENELAUS

What have we done to him that I should suffer for it?

DOORKEEPER

It is because Zeus' daughter, Helen, is in this house.   470

MENELAUS

What? What is this you are telling me? Say it again.

DOORKEEPER

I mean Tyndareus' daughter who lived in Sparta once.

MENELAUS

Where did she come from? What is the explanation of this?

DOORKEEPER

She came from Lacedaemon and made her way here.

MENELAUS

When? Has my wife I left in the cave been carried off?   475

DOORKEEPER

She came, stranger, before the Achaeans sailed for Troy.
But go away from here quietly. The state of things
inside is such that all the great house is upside down.
You came at the wrong time, and if my master catches
you, all the hospitality you will find is death.   480
I myself like the Greeks, in spite of those harsh words
I gave you. I was afraid of what my master might do.

(The Doorkeeper goes back into the palace and closes the door.)

MENELAUS

What am I to think or make of this? She tells me now
of present difficulties after those gone by,
since, while I come bringing my wife, lost once by force,   485
from Troy, and she is guarded for me in the cave,

all the while some other woman with the same name
as my wife has been living in this house. She said
that this one was by birth the child of Zeus. Can it be
there is some man who bears the name of Zeus and lives   490
beside the banks of the Nile? No, there's one Zeus; in heaven.
And where on earth is Sparta except only where
Eurotas' waters ripple by the lovely reeds?
Tyndareus is a famous name. There is only one.
And where is there another land called Lacedaemon   495
or Troy either? I do not know what to make of it.
I suppose it must be that in the wide world a great many
have the same name, men named like other men, cities
like cities, women like women. Nothing to wonder at
in this.

      I will not run away for the servant's threats.   500
There is no man whose heart is so uncivilized
that when he has heard my name he will not give me food.
Troy is renowned, and I, who lit the fire of Troy,°
Menelaus, am not unknown anywhere in all
the world. I will await the master of the house. I have   505
a choice of courses. If he is a savage man
I will hide myself and make for where I left the wreck,
but if he gives way and is gentle, I shall ask
for what the present circumstances make me need.
Of all the evils in my distressed plight, this is   510
the worst, that I, myself a king, should have to ask
other kings for sustenance. But so it has to be.
For the saying is not mine, but it was wisely said,
that nothing has more strength than dire necessity.

                    (Enter the Chorus and Helen from the palace.)

CHORUS [*singing*]
  Before I came back I heard from the maid   515
  prophetic all she divined for the house
  of kings: how Menelaus is not
  lost yet nor sunk in the dim,

shining cave of the under-earth,
but still over the sea's surges 520
hard driven he cannot win
to the harbors of his own land,
in hardship, wandering
for want of food, with his friends all gone
all across the wide world he keeps 525
his foot hard for the oarsman's stroke
since ever he sailed from Troy land.

HELEN [*speaking*]

So, here am I, come back to the shelter of the tomb
once more. I have heard Theonoë's words, and they were good,
and she knows everything. She says my husband lives° 530
still in the light and looks upon the day-star; yet
he is driven sailing back and forth along the sea
on endless crossings, hardened by the wanderer's life,
but when his work is ended and over, he will come.
One thing she did not tell me, if after he returns 535
he will be safe. I carefully did not ask her this,
I was so happy to hear that he is safe so far.
She said also that he was in this country, near
at hand, a shipwrecked castaway with just few friends.
When will you come? And if you come, how dear to me! 540

(*She catches sight of Menelaus.*)

Who is it, who are you? Does this mean I am waylaid
by the machinations of Proteus' godless son? What shall
I do? Not run like a racing filly, like the god's
Bacchant, up to the tomb with flying feet? This man
is savage by his look and hunts me for his prey. 545

MENELAUS

You, who now race in such an agony of fear
to reach the grave mound and the uprights where the fires
are burned, stay! Why this flight? Know, when I saw your face
it struck me with amazement and with disbelief.

HELEN

    We are set upon, my women. This man bars my way   550
    to the tomb. His purpose is to catch me, and then give
    me over to that tyrant whose embrace I shun.

MENELAUS

    I am no thief, nor any servant of bad men.

HELEN

    And yet the clothes that cover you are poor and mean.

MENELAUS

    Stay your swift feet from running, put aside your fear.   555

HELEN

    Very well, I will stand, since I have reached the tomb.°

MENELAUS

    Who are you? I look, lady, upon your face: whose face?

HELEN

    And who are you? The same question for both of us.

MENELAUS

    Never have I seen a form so like another form.

HELEN

    Oh gods!—it is divine to recognize your own.   560

MENELAUS

    Are you a Hellene woman or a native here?°

HELEN

    Hellene. But tell me who you are. I would know too.

MENELAUS

    You are more like Helen, my lady, than any I know.

HELEN

    You are like Menelaus, too. What does it mean?

MENELAUS

    The truth. You have recognized this most unhappy man.   565

HELEN

Oh, you are come at long last here to your wife's arms.

MENELAUS

Wife? What wife do you mean? Take your hands off my
clothes.

HELEN

The wife Tyndareus, my own father, gave to you.

MENELAUS

O Hecate of the lights, send better dreams than this.

HELEN

It's not a phantom-slave of the crossway goddess you see.   570

MENELAUS

I am only one man and could not have two wives.

HELEN

And who might be the other wife whose lord you are?

MENELAUS

She whom the cave hides, whom I brought from the Phrygian
land.

HELEN

I am your wife. There is no other in my place.

MENELAUS

Am I in my right mind? Or are my eyes at fault?   575

HELEN

When you look at me, do you not think you see your wife?

MENELAUS

Your body is like hers. Certainty fails me.

HELEN

                                        Look and see.
What more do you want? And who knows me better than you?

MENELAUS

In very truth you are like her. That I will not deny.

HELEN

What better teacher shall you have than your own eyes? 580

MENELAUS

But here's my problem: that another is my wife.

HELEN

It was an image of me. I never went to Troy.

MENELAUS

And what artificer makes bodies live and breathe?

HELEN

The air: from which the work of gods shaped you a bride.

MENELAUS

And which of the gods made her? This is past all wit. 585

HELEN

It was Hera made the switch, so Paris should not have me.

MENELAUS

How could you be here and in Troy at the same time?

HELEN

A name can be in many places, the body not.

MENELAUS

Let me go. I had pain enough when I came here.

HELEN

And will you leave me, for that empty shadow's arms? 590

MENELAUS

You are like Helen, so, at least, happy farewell.

HELEN

Lost, lost! I won my husband, and must lose him still.

MENELAUS

I trust my memory of great hardships more than you.

HELEN

Ah me, was any woman more wretched ever? They
who stand closest forsake me. I shall never find   595
my way to Greece, my native country, ever again.

(Enter Servant of Menelaus from the side.)

SERVANT

Menelaus, I have been wandering all over this land
of barbarians looking for you and find you now
at last. The friends you left behind sent me for you.

MENELAUS

What is it? Have the barbarians robbed or plundered you?   600

SERVANT

A strange thing, stranger in itself than the telling of it.

MENELAUS

Tell me. You must bring some surprise, for haste like this.

SERVANT

I tell you: all your thousand toils were toiled in vain.

MENELAUS

This is old weeping for old sorrows. What is new?

SERVANT

Your wife is gone, swept up and away and out of sight   605
into the hollows of the high air. Sky veils her now.
She left the secret cave where we were keeping her
with only this said to us: "Wretched men of Troy
and all you Achaeans who, day after day, went on
dying for me beside Scamander, by Hera's craft,   610
you thought Paris had Helen, when he never did.
Now I, having kept the duty of destiny, and stayed
the time I had to stay, go back into the sky,

my father. All for nothing Tyndareus' daughter has
heard evil things said of her, who did nothing wrong." 615
      Oh, daughter of Leda, hail! Were you here all this time?
I was in the act of telling him, fool that I was,
how you had left our caverns for the stars and gone
on wings away. I will not let you mock at us
like this again. It was enough hardship that you 620
gave to your husband and his helpers there in Troy.

MENELAUS

I see it, I see it! All the story that she told
has come out true. O day of my desires, that gives
you back into my arms to take and hold again!

HELEN°

Oh, dearest of men to me, Menelaus, time has grown 625
old, but the joy that now is ours is fresh and new.

[*singing throughout the following interchange while Menelaus
alternates between speaking and singing*]
*I have my husband again, all my delight, sweet friends,
my arms circle him now,
beloved, light and a flame in dark that has been so long.*

MENELAUS [*speaking*]

And I hold you. And we have so much to say about 630
the time between, I do not know where to begin.

HELEN

*I am so happy, all my hair is rising
with shivering pleasure, and the tears burst. Husband
and love, I have your body here close in my arms,
happiness, mine again.* 635

MENELAUS [*singing*]

*O sweetest face, there is nothing left to wish for.
This is my bride, daughter of Zeus and Leda.°*

HELEN

She whom the boys of white horses, boys of my bloodline
brought by torchlight, to bless me, to bless me . . .   640

MENELAUS

. . . long ago, but it was a god who took you away
from my house, and drove you
away, where your fate was the stronger.

HELEN

But evil turned to good brought us together again,
my husband, lost so long. Now may my luck be good.   645

MENELAUS [*speaking*]

May it be good, surely. All my prayer is as your prayer.
Where there are two, one cannot be wretched, and one not.

HELEN

My friends, dear friends, I will no longer
weep and grieve for the past.
I have my husband, I have him. Long I waited for him,   650
all the years of Troy, waited for him to come.

MENELAUS

You have me, I have you. But the suns of ten thousand days
were hard to win through to god's gladness here at the end.

HELEN

My happiness has its tears in it; but there is more
sweetness here than the pain.   655

MENELAUS

What shall I say? Who ever could hope that this would be?

HELEN

I have you so unhoped-for here against my breasts!

MENELAUS [*singing*]

And I hold you, when I thought you had gone away
to Idaean Troy and to those pitiful towers.

[speaking]
In gods' name, tell me how you were taken from my house.   660

HELEN

Ah, a bitter cause that you open here,
and ah, a bitter story you waken for me.

MENELAUS

Speak. The gods gave this; we must even hear it out.

HELEN

I spit away that story, the story that I must tell.

MENELAUS

Tell it still. There is pleasure in hardships heard about.   665

HELEN

It was not to the bed of a young barbarian man
borne on the beating of oars,
borne on the beating of desire for a lawless love.

MENELAUS

No, but what spirit, what destiny robbed home of you?°

HELEN

The son of Zeus, of Zeus and of Maia,° my lord,   670
brought me here to the Nile.

MENELAUS

Strange, strange! Who sent him? There is wonder in this tale.

HELEN

I have wept for this; my eyes are wet with tears.
It was the wife of Zeus destroyed me.

MENELAUS

Hera? What need had she to give this evil to us?   675

HELEN

Ah, there was danger for me in the bathing there and the springs
where the goddesses made bright
their bodies; there the judgment was begun.

MENELAUS

And Hera made the judgment mean this evil for you?°

HELEN

So she might take away from Paris . . .

MENELAUS [*singing*]

How? Speak. 680

HELEN

. . . me. Cypris had promised him me.

MENELAUS

Oh, poor woman.

HELEN

Cruel, cruel. So I was driven to Egypt.

MENELAUS [*speaking*]

She gave him the image in your place. So you tell me.

HELEN

*But you in your house, my mother, ah, the sorrows of you,
the hurt that happened.*

MENELAUS [*singing*]

Tell me. 685

HELEN

*My mother is gone. Ill-starred in my marriage
and for my shame she caught the noose to her neck.*

MENELAUS [*speaking*]

Ah. But Hermione our daughter, does she live?

HELEN

*Wedless, childless, my dear, she grieves
for my marriage that was none.*° 690

MENELAUS

Oh, Paris, you destroyed my house from top to bottom!

HELEN

This killed you too, and in their thousands killed
the bronze-armored Danaans.
It was the god who cast me away from my city, from you,
out of the land of my fathers, star-crossed and cursed   695
when I left my house, when I left my bed
—but I left them not for a shameful love!

CHORUS LEADER

If now for the rest of fortune you are fortunate,
in time to come, it is enough to heal the past.

SERVANT

Menelaus, let me into your happiness as well.   700
I am listening to it too, but still I am not clear.

MENELAUS

Indeed, dear old man. Share in what we have to say.

SERVANT

Did she not cause the sorrows for the men in Troy?

MENELAUS

She did not. We were swindled by the gods. We had°
our hands upon an idol made of clouds.

SERVANT

                              You mean   705
it was for a cloud, for nothing, we did all that work?

MENELAUS

The hand of Hera, the strife of the three goddesses.

SERVANT

This woman who stands here with us is your real wife?

MENELAUS

Herself. It is I who tell you this. You must believe.   710

SERVANT

My daughter, the way of god is complex; he is hard

for us to predict. He moves the pieces and they come
somehow into a kind of order. Some have bad luck°
while others, scatheless, meet their evil and go down
in turn. None can hold fortune still and make it last.   715
You and your husband have had your turn of trouble now.
Yours was a story, but he fought with the spear, and all
his hard fighting was fought for nothing. Now his luck
has turned, and the highest blessings fall into his hands.
You never shamed your aged father, never shamed   720
your divine brothers, nor did what you were rumored to.
It all comes back to me, your marriage long ago,
and I remember the torch I carried as I ran
beside your four-horse chariot, where you, a bride,
rode from your noble house beside the master here.   725
He is a poor thing who does not feel as his masters do,
grieve in their grief, be happy in their happiness.
I, though I wear the name of servant, yet aspire°
to be counted in the number of the generous
slaves, for I do not have the name of liberty   730
but have the heart. Better this, than for a single man
to have the double evil of an evil spirit
and to be named by those about him as a slave.

MENELAUS

Come then, old friend, you who have had your share of work
in the hard toils beneath the shield and at my side,   735
share now the blessings of my fortune too, and go
to take the news back to those friends I left behind—
how you have found our state here, how our luck holds now;
tell them, too, to wait by the seashore, follow from there
the progress of those trials of strength I see in store   740
for me, and if we can steal my wife out of this place
they must see to it that, joining our fortunes all in one,
we get clear of these barbarians, if we have the strength.

SERVANT

It shall be done, my lord.

                                              Only, now I am sure
how rotten this business of prophets is, how full of lies.   745
There never was any good in burning things on fires°
nor in the voices of fowl. It is sheer idiocy
even to think that birds do people any good.
Calchas said nothing about this; he never told
the army when he saw his friends die for a cloud,   750
nor Helenus either, and a city was stormed in vain.
You might say: "No, for god did not wish it that way."°
Then why consult the prophets? We should sacrifice
to the gods, ask them for blessings, and let prophecy go.
The art was invented as a bait for making money,   755
but no lazy man gets rich just by burnt offerings.
The best prophet is common sense and thoughtful planning.

                                              (*Exit to the side.*)

CHORUS LEADER

My own opinion about prophets tallies with
that of this old man. If you have the gods for friends
you have a better thing than prophecy for your house.   760

HELEN [*now speaking*]

So. All is well now here where I have been. But tell
me, my poor husband, how you survived Troy. I know
there's no gain in my learning, but when you love you feel
a fascination in even the sorrows of those you love.

MENELAUS

Your single question, one approach, asks me so much.   765
Why must I tell you how the Aegean wore us out,
of the Euboean wrecking-fires Nauplius set,
of Crete, of the Libyan cities we were driven upon,
of Perseus' watchtower? Even could I satisfy
you telling of troubles, telling would only burden me   770
who am so tired already, and be double pain.

HELEN

What you have said was much more than my question. Still,

leave out the rest and tell me only this. How long
have you been wandering battered on the waves of the sea?

MENELAUS

The years at Troy were ten, and to this add the time   775
I was at sea, where I filled the circles of seven years.

HELEN

Too long, unhappy husband, all too long a time
to live through, and survive it, and come here to die.

MENELAUS

To die! What will you tell me now? You have broken me.

HELEN

Make your escape, get clear of this place with speed, or else°   780
you will be killed by the man who is the master here.

MENELAUS

What have I done to deserve treatment such as this?

HELEN

You have come unlooked-for to prevent my marrying.

MENELAUS

You mean someone here is trying to marry my wife?

HELEN

He meant to force my favors; and I must endure.   785

MENELAUS

In his own private strength, or by some lordship here?

HELEN

The man is Proteus' son and master of the land.

MENELAUS

Now this then was the puzzle of what the doorkeeper said.

HELEN

At what barbarian doors have you been standing now?

MENELAUS

These. And like any beggar I was driven away. 790

HELEN

You were not asking for charity? Oh, my shame.

MENELAUS

The action was that, but I did not call it so.

HELEN

It seems, then, you know all about his courting me.

MENELAUS

I know; what I do not know is whether you held him off.

HELEN

Hear it then: all my love is kept untouched for you. 795

MENELAUS

What will make me sure of this? But how sweet, if true!

HELEN

Do you see where I sat in suffering beside this tomb?

MENELAUS

I see your wretched pallet. What was your plan?

HELEN

I took a suppliant's place here to escape his bed.

MENELAUS

For lack of an altar, or is it the barbarians' custom here? 800

HELEN

It saved me, as well as the gods' temples could have done.

MENELAUS

Is there no way for me and my ship to take you home?

HELEN

A sword waits for you, rather than a love-bed with me.

MENELAUS

Thus I would be the most unhappy man alive.

HELEN

Take flight, and do not be ashamed. Escape from here.   805

MENELAUS

And leave you? It was for your sake I captured Troy.

HELEN

But better so than that my love should mean your death.

MENELAUS

Cowardly counsel, unworthy of the siege of Troy.

HELEN

You would kill the king, I suspect. It cannot be done.

MENELAUS

You mean he has a body that no steel can pierce?   810

HELEN

You will see. A wise man doesn't attempt what can't be done.

MENELAUS

Shall I then quietly give him my hands to tie?

HELEN

You are desperate. What we need now is strategy.

MENELAUS

I would rather die in action than die in doing nothing.

HELEN

There is a single hope for escape, a single way.   815

MENELAUS

What way? Bribery? Daring and force? Or argument?

HELEN

What if the tyrant never learns that you are here?

MENELAUS

Who will tell him? He will not know me by himself.

HELEN

He has an ally, strong as a god, inside the house.

MENELAUS

Some voice has come and taken a secret place inside?   820

HELEN

No, it is his sister, whom they call Theonoë.

MENELAUS

The name is prophetic, surely. Tell me what she does.

HELEN

She knows everything. She will tell her brother you are here.

MENELAUS

That would be death. I have no way to stay concealed.

HELEN

But if we threw ourselves on her mercy, worked on her . . .   825

MENELAUS

To do what? What is the hope you lead me gently to?

HELEN

. . . so she won't tell her brother you are in the land.

MENELAUS

If we won her over, could we get ourselves out of here?

HELEN

With her help, easily. Without her knowledge, no.

MENELAUS

Best for woman to approach woman. You do this.   830

HELEN

She will not leave until my arms have embraced her knees.

MENELAUS

But look now. What if she will not listen to us?

HELEN

You must die, and I be married by force, and sorrowful.

MENELAUS

But betraying me still. By force, you say. Just an excuse.

HELEN

No, then. I have sworn a sacred oath, by your own head.   835

MENELAUS

You mean that you will die and never change your husband?

HELEN

Die by the sword that kills you, and be laid to rest
beside you.

MENELAUS

I accept it. Take my hand on this.

HELEN

I take it, and swear to forsake the daylight if you die.

MENELAUS

And I swear, if I lose you I shall take my life.   840

HELEN

How, in such death, shall we make men know how we died?

MENELAUS

I will kill you on this grave mound, then kill myself.
But come, first I shall dare a great action for your sake
and for our marriage. Whoever wants you, let him come.
I will not shame my glories from the Trojan War   845
nor take the common blame of Hellas when I come home,
I who made Thetis lose Achilles, I who looked
on Telamonian Ajax in his suicide
and saw Nestor made childless. Shall I then not dare

count death as worth the dying for my lady's sake?   850
Oh, I must. If there are gods and if they are wise,
when a man falls high-hearted at the hands of enemies
they make the earth lie light upon him in the grave,
but fling the cowards out on the hard stones of earth.

CHORUS LEADER

Oh gods, I pray you, let the race of Tantalus   855
turn fortunate at last, and let their troubles end.

HELEN

Unhappy me! My destiny is luckless still.
Menelaus, we have no chance left. Theonoë
the diviner is coming out now, for the house sounds
to the unbarring of the doors. Run! Only where   860
to run? What use? Whether or not she is here, she knows
that you are here. Poor me, it is surely ruin now.
And you, saved from barbarian Troy, you have come here
once again to be slain by a barbarian sword.

(Enter Theonoë from the palace, attended by two servants.)

THEONOË

You, lead the way. Bear gleaming torches, and fumigate   865
the furthest reach of heaven, following holy law,
so we may take and breathe the purity of this air.
And you: if anyone with unhallowed foot has stepped
and fouled the way, treat it with purifying flame,
strike with the torch so I can make my way through. Then   870
when we have rendered our devotion to the gods
take the fire back inside to burn upon the hearth.

(The servants do as instructed, then exit into the palace.)

Helen, what of my prophecies? Are they not true?
Here is your husband Menelaus, plain before
my eyes, with his ships lost, and with your image gone.   875
Poor man, with what dangers escaped you have come here,
nor even yet know whether you shall go home or must

stay here. This very day before the seat of Zeus
there shall be quarreling among the gods about
your case. Hera, who was your enemy before   880
but is now your friend, desires that you go home with Helen
here, so that Greece may learn how Aphrodite's gift
to Alexander of a bride was a false gift.
Cypris would wreck your homecoming, so none shall know
the truth of how she bought the name of beauty for   885
false payment, Helen's marriage—which was no real thing.
The decision rests with me, to do as Cypris wills
and tell my brother you are here, destroy you so,
or take the side of Hera, save your life, and hide
your coming from my brother, though his orders were   890
to tell him, when your journey home brought you this way.

Which of you will go tell my brother that this man°
is here? Thus will my welfare be made safe for me.

(Helen kneels at the feet of Theonoë.)

HELEN

Maiden, I throw myself as suppliant upon
your knees, and kneel in a forlorn posture, for the sake   895
of my own self and for this man. I have found him
at last, and finding him am like to see him die.
Do not then tell your brother that my husband here
has come to my most loving and beloved arms,
but save him, I implore you. You must not betray   900
your duty and your good name for your brother's sake
to buy him wicked pleasures he does not deserve.
God hates violence. He has ordained that all men
fairly acquire their property, not seize it. So
wealth obtained unjustly must be left alone.°   905
There is the sky, which is all men's together; there
is the world to live in, fill with houses of our own
nor hold another's, nor tear it from his hands by force.
For me it was hard, and yet it was a timely thing,

that Hermes gave me to your father to keep safe   910
for my husband, who is here and who would have me back.
How can he take me back when he is dead? And how°
could your brother duly give the living to the dead?
Consider now your father's case, consider god's.
Would the divine power, and would the dead man, wish to see   915
what belongs to another given back, or would they not?
I think they would. You must not give a greater weight
to a wild brother than to an honorable father.
If you, who are a prophetess and understand
the gods' concerns, will spoil the just actions of your father   920
and uphold the right of an unrighteous brother, then
to know the gods' concerns is a disgraceful thing.
Shame to know past and future, not know right and wrong!
And me, surrounded as I am by miseries—
save me and add that bonus to your act of justice.   925
There is no man living but Helen is his hate,
notorious through all Hellas as having betrayed
my husband, to live in the Phrygians' golden houses.
But if I go to Greece and reach Sparta again
and they hear, and see, how it was by the arts of gods   930
that they were ruined, that I never betrayed my loves,
they will restore me to my reputation once
again. My daughter—nobody will take her now—
will be betrothed by me. I'll escape the homeless life
I lead here, and live on my own money in my own house.   935
If Menelaus lay dead and murdered° on the pyre,
I should have loved him from a distance, with my tears.
But he is here, alive. Must he be taken from me?

No, maiden, no. I kneel here as your suppliant.
Give me your grace in this, and let your ways be like   940
your upright father's ways, for it is the brightest fame
of children, when they have a father who was good,
if they can match the character that gave them birth.

CHORUS LEADER

The words you have spoken now are truly pitiful
and you are pitiable too. Yet still, I long to hear   945
what Menelaus has to argue for his life.

MENELAUS

I cannot bring myself to fall before your feet
nor to make my eyes wet with tears. Such abjectness
would be the greatest shame upon the tale of Troy.
Yet some assert, or so I've heard, that noble men   950
in times of woe will let the tears pour from their eyes.
I waive this privilege of honor—if privilege
of honor it is. Courage is better.

                                                        Rather, thus:
if you think best to save a man, a visitor,
who asks with right to have his wife given back to him,   955
give her, and save me too. If you do not think it best,
it does not mean new misery for me but the old
continued; and it means you are an evil woman.
But what I think is worthy and right for me to say,
and what will touch your heart beyond all else, I shall   960
say kneeling here before your father's tomb, in grief.

Aged sir, who dwell here in the stony tomb,
give her back to me. What I ask is my own wife
whom Zeus had brought here, so you could keep her safe
    for me.
I understand now you will never give her back   965
since you are dead. But this lady here must not approve
that her invoked and famous father underground shall hear
despiteful speech against him. All is in her hands.

Hades of the downworld, I invoke your aid as well.
You have taken many dead men, fallen before my sword,   970
because of this woman. You are paid your price in full.
Now bring these bodies to life again and yield them back,

or force this maiden now to match her father's fame
for pious dealing, and give back my bride to me.
If you Egyptians take my wife away from me,   975
I will tell you what will happen then, as she did not.
For your attention, maiden: we are bound by oath.
First I shall find your brother and we two shall fight.
He will be killed, or I. There is no more to say.
But if he lacks the courage to stand up to me,   980
and tries to starve and snare two suppliants at the tomb,
I have decided to kill her, then thrust the blade
of this two-edged sword into my own heart, upon
the back of this grave mound before us, where the blood
will splash and drip upon the grave. There we shall lie   985
two corpses, side by side, upon the marble tomb,
to shame your father, to pain you, for evermore.
Your brother will not marry her. Nobody else
will marry her. I shall take her away with me,
away to the dead, if I cannot bring her home.   990

Why do I say this? Turning to woman and to tears°
I should be pitied, but I should get nothing done.
Kill me, if you think best. You will not kill your shame.
But better, be persuaded by my arguments;
for so you would be just, and I should have my wife.   995

CHORUS LEADER
   It is yours to pass judgment on their arguments,
   maiden. Judge then, and judge so all will be well pleased.

THEONOË
   My nature is to be pious; so is my wish.
   I have myself to think of, and my father's name
   is not to be defiled. I must not give my brother   1000
   such pleasures as will leave me with my honor gone.
   The sanctity of justice is a powerful thing
   in my own nature. This is Nereus' heritage.
   I have it, Menelaus; I will try to keep

it always. And, since Hera wishes to help you, 1005
my vote shall be as Hera votes. And as for Cypris
(may she not be offended!), that means nothing here.
My aim is to remain a virgin all my life.°
As for reproaches on my father and this tomb,
the same tale must apply to me. I would do wrong 1010
not to restore her. For my father, had he lived,
would have given her back to you, and you to her.

      For all men, in the world below and in the world
above, must pay for acts committed here. The mind
of those who have died, blown into the immortal air, 1015
immortally keeps knowledge, though all life is gone.
I must not strain this matter to great length. I shall
be quiet about your supplication, and shall not
let my good counsels help my brother toward his lust.
Really, I serve him so, though he might not think so, 1020
if I can make him good, not dissolute any more.
Now it will rest upon yourselves to find a way.
I shall have nothing to do with it, but shall withdraw
and be silent. Begin by praying to the gods, and ask
the Lady of Cyprus to let Helen now come home, 1025
and ask Hera to hold steadfastly that good will
toward you, and toward your husband, which shall save you
    both.

My father, you are dead, but while I have the strength
your name of piety shall not change to an impious name.

                     (Exit into the palace.)

CHORUS LEADER
  The unrighteous are never really fortunate. 1030
  Our hopes for safety depend upon our doing right.

HELEN
  We are safe, Menelaus, as far as the maiden is concerned.
  Now it's up to us to propose measures, so that we
  can make a plan between us to escape from here.

MENELAUS

Listen then: you have lived some time in this house   1035
and have been familiar with the attendants of the king.

HELEN

Yes, but why did you mention it? Does it mean you hope
to accomplish something that will help the two of us?

MENELAUS

Would you be able to persuade those who have charge
of the chariots? Would they perhaps give us one?   1040

HELEN

I could persuade them. But what use? How shall we flee
the plains of this strange land where we do not know our
    way?

MENELAUS

Hopeless, as you say ... Come, then, hide me in the house
and I'll kill the king with my own blade. Shall we do this?

HELEN

No. His sister could no longer keep the secret   1045
of your presence here, if it were to mean her brother's death.

MENELAUS

But we have no ship in which to make a safe escape.
The ship we had is at the bottom of the sea.

HELEN

Listen! Even a woman can have a clever thought.
Are you willing, though not dead, to be reported dead?   1050

MENELAUS

Unlucky omen. But if it does us any good
I consent. You may say that I am dead, though I am not.

HELEN

Then we shall use the pitiful customs of women,
the dirges and cutting of hair, against that impious man.

MENELAUS

Where is there any help toward our escape in this?   1055
I think that what you say is rather obsolete.

HELEN

Well, then I'll say that you have died at sea, and ask
the king to let me bury you in effigy.

MENELAUS

Suppose he grants it? Even so, without a ship,
how shall we save our bodies by this cenotaph?   1060

HELEN

I shall ask him for a boat, so that your burial
fineries may be submerged and gathered in the sea's arms.

MENELAUS

Well spoken, except for one thing. He will merely say
you must bury him on land. Where, then, is your excuse?

HELEN

But I shall tell him that in Greece it is not allowed   1065
to bury ashore those who have met their death at sea.

MENELAUS

Right again; so you correct things. Then I too shall sail
in the same boat, and with you cast the offerings down.

HELEN

By all means, yes, you are to be there. Bring with you
those mariners of yours who escaped from the shipwreck.   1070

MENELAUS

Thus once I get possession of the anchored ship
they will be ready, man by man, their swords in hand.

HELEN

You shall be in charge of all thenceforward. Only let
the wind blow fair in our sails. Let the ship run!

MENELAUS

It shall. The gods will end my troubles now at last.   1075
Who will you say has told you the story of my death?

HELEN

You. And you tell him you sailed with Atreus' son, and that
you were the sole survivor, and you saw him die.

MENELAUS

This fishing net of rags I wear upon my body
will be convincing proof of my shipwrecked condition.   1080

HELEN

Yes, this is timely now, though then it seemed untimely.
The misery of that moment might now turn into good.

MENELAUS

Should I then go inside the house with you, or sit
here and wait quietly for you beside the tomb?

HELEN

Stay here. So, if he uses violence on you   1085
this tomb, and then your own sword, will be your defense.
I shall go in the house and cut my curls and change
the white clothing that I wear for black, and drag
my nails across my cheek leaving a red furrow there.
I must. Great hazard. I see two ways the scales can tip.   1090
I may be caught in trickery, then I must die.
Or I shall save your life, and we shall both go home.
O queen and goddess, given to the arms of Zeus,
Hera! We are two pitiful people. Grant us release
from toils. We ask, and lift our arms straight toward that sky   1095
where your home is, among the splendors of the stars.
And you, who won that beauty contest by my marriage,
you, Dione's daughter, Cypris, destroy me not.
It is enough, that filth you rolled me in before
when you gave barbarians not my body but my name.   1100
But if you wish to kill me, let me only die

in my own country. Why this thirst for evil things?
Why do you work in passions, lies, devices full
of treachery, love magics, murder in the home?
Were you only temperate, in all else you are found sweet   1105
to us beyond all other gods. This I confess.

(*Exit into the palace.*)

CHORUS [*singing*]

STROPHE A

To you, who deep forested, choired in the growth
of singing wood hide nested,
to you I utter my outcry,
to you, beyond all other birds sweet in your singing,
O nightingale of the sorrows,   1110
come, with brown beak trilling,
to the beat of your melody, come
with song to my sad singing
as I mourn for the hard sorrows
of Helen, for all the suffering,
all the tears of the daughters of Troy   1115
from spears held by Achaeans,
all from the time when with barbarian oar he swept over
the water-flats, came, came, and his coming was sorrow
in marriage for Priam's people, moving
from Lacedaemon, from you, Helen: Paris, dark lover   1120
brought there by Aphrodite.

ANTISTROPHE A

And there were many Achaeans who by the spear
and by the stone's smash have died
and are given grimly to Hades.
For these, unhappy wives have cut their long hair.
The chambers of their love are left forsaken.   1125
Many others besides were drowned
by an Achaean, that man of the single oar,
off waterswept Euboea

[67]   HELEN

when he lit his wreck fires, blazed
the false flares, and crashed them to death
on Aegean rocks at Caphereus.   1130
And for Menelaus, the harborless mountains in the storm wind°
were death, when he was driven far from his homeland,
carrying the prize of his barbarian glory;
prize, no prize, but war,
the Greek cloud shape his ship carried off,   1135
the sacred image Hera made.

STROPHE B

What is god, what is not god, what is between man
and god, who shall say? I'd say he has found
the remote way to the absolute,
he who sees the gods' concerns coming   1140
here to us, then returning there, and coming
back again, leaping
to unexpected fortunes.
Yourself were born, Helen, daughter to Zeus.
Winged in the curves of Leda there   1145
as bird he fathered you.
Yet even you are denounced through Greece
as traitress, faithless, rightless, godless. No man's°
thought I can speak of is ever clear,
no word about gods have I found unbroken.   1150

ANTISTROPHE B

Mindless, all of you, who in the strength of spears
and the tearing edge win your valors
by war, thus stupidly gaining
freedom from pains in death.
For if bloody debate shall settle   1155
the issue, never again
shall hate be gone out of the cities of men.
By hate they won the chambers of Priam's city;°
they could have resolved by reason and words
the quarrel, Helen, for you.   1160

Now these are given to the Death God below.
On the walls the flame, as of Zeus, lightened and fell.°
And you, Helen, upon your sorrows bear
more hardships still, and more matter for grieving.

(Enter Theoclymenus from the side, attended by hunters.)

THEOCLYMENUS

Tomb of my father, greeting! It was even for such   1165
addresses, Proteus, I caused you to be buried here
at the entrance, and in passing in and out of doors
I, Theoclymenus your son, greet you, Father.
You, my serving men, take the dogs and the hunting nets
inside the king's palace; put them away.

(The servants do as instructed.)

                                      Now I   1170
have found many hard things to say against myself.
Do we not chastise evildoers with death? And yet
even now they tell me there has been a Greek man seen
who has openly come here but has escaped the guards,
to spy on us, or watching for the chance to steal   1175
Helen away. Let him be caught, and he is dead.
Ah,
I have come too late, it seems. The whole thing has been done
and the daughter of Tyndareus, leaving empty her place
in the tomb's shelter, is carried away out of the land.
Hallo! Unbar all bolts and let the horses out   1180
from their mangers, men, and get the chariots out and ready.
Let it not be for lack of effort that the bride
I would win is stolen secretly from my domain.

(Enter Helen from the palace.)

No, wait. I see the ones that I am after, here
beside the palace still, they have not yet escaped.   1185
Why have you changed from your white clothes, and put on
    black

and wear them? Why have you put the iron blade to your head
and shorn away the glory of your lovely hair?
And why are your cheeks wet with the fresh tears? For whom
do you weep? Is it compulsion of dreams in the night   1190
that makes you sorrow so, or have you heard from home
some rumor, and the grief of it has wrecked your heart?

HELEN

My lord—for now at last I name you in such terms—
my life is ruined. There is nothing left for me.

THEOCLYMENUS

What has happened? What is the disaster that has struck you
down?   1195

HELEN

My Menelaus—how shall I say it? He is dead.

THEOCLYMENUS

I cannot take pleasure in what you tell me, though it is
my fortune.° How do you know? Did Theonoë tell you?

HELEN

She says so. Also, one who was with him when he died.

THEOCLYMENUS

There is someone here then, with an authentic report?   1200

HELEN

Yes, here. May he go to where I wish him to go!

THEOCLYMENUS

Who is he? Where is he? Tell me, let me get this clear.

HELEN

That man you see there, sitting abject under the tomb.

THEOCLYMENUS

By Apollo! The rags of clothing he is in!

HELEN

I think my husband has looked thus. I pity both.   1205

THEOCLYMENUS

Who is this man? Where from? Where did he come ashore?

HELEN

He is a Greek, an Achaean who sailed with my husband.

THEOCLYMENUS

What manner of death does he say that Menelaus died?

HELEN

The most pitiful; washed down in the running sea.

THEOCLYMENUS

Where in barbarian waters was he sailing then? 1210

HELEN

He was driven against Libya's harborless cliffs.

THEOCLYMENUS

How was this man his oarsmate, and yet did not die?

HELEN

Sometimes the baser have more fortune than their betters.

THEOCLYMENUS

He is here, a castaway. Where did he leave his ship?

HELEN

Where I wish he had perished, and Menelaus had not. 1215

THEOCLYMENUS

But Menelaus is dead. In what boat did this man come?

HELEN

Sailors came on him and picked him up, or so he says.

THEOCLYMENUS

Where is that evil that was brought to Troy instead of you?

HELEN

The cloud image? You mean that? Gone into the sky.

THEOCLYMENUS

O Priam, O Troy, how you were brought down in vain! 1220

HELEN

I too, with Priam's children, shared this luckless chance.

THEOCLYMENUS

Did he leave your husband unburied? Is he beneath ground?

HELEN

Not buried yet. And oh, my grief!

THEOCLYMENUS

Was it for this
you cut away the long curls of your yellow hair?

HELEN

He is dear to me even now just as he was before.°   1225

THEOCLYMENUS

This is real. Sorrow has distracted her to tears.°

HELEN

It could easily happen that your sister might be fooled.°

THEOCLYMENUS

Oh, no. How?
Will you go on making this tomb your home?

HELEN

Why do you make fun of me? Let the dead man be.

THEOCLYMENUS

Yet you show faith to him when you keep far from me.   1230

HELEN

That is all past. You may make the wedding arrangements
now.

THEOCLYMENUS

It has been long in coming, but I still am glad.

HELEN

Do you know what we should do? Let us forget the past.

THEOCLYMENUS

On what terms? Grace should be given in return for grace.

HELEN

Let us make peace between ourselves. Forgive me all.   1235

THEOCLYMENUS

My quarrel with you is canceled. Let it go with the wind.

HELEN

But by your knees I ask of you, if you are my friend . . .

THEOCLYMENUS

What is it that your suppliant arms would wrest from me?

HELEN

I desire your permission to bury my dead lord.

THEOCLYMENUS

How? Are there graves for the lost? Would you bury a
shadow?   1240

HELEN

There is a Greek custom for those who die at sea . . .

THEOCLYMENUS

What is it? Pelops' people are knowing in such things.

HELEN

. . . to hold a burial ceremony in empty robes.

THEOCLYMENUS

Do it, then. Raise a mound on my land, where you wish.

HELEN

It is not thus we bury our drowned mariners.   1245

THEOCLYMENUS

How, then? I am not expert in Greek usages.

HELEN

We take all that the dead should be given out to sea.

THEOCLYMENUS

What shall I give you for your dead, then?

HELEN

This man knows.
I am inexperienced. All my luck was good before.

THEOCLYMENUS

So, friend, you have brought me news that I am glad to hear.   1250

MENELAUS

Not good hearing for me, nor for the dead.

THEOCLYMENUS

Tell me,
how do you bury those who have been drowned at sea?

MENELAUS

As lavishly as a man's substance lets him do.

THEOCLYMENUS

For this woman's sake tell me without minding the cost.

MENELAUS

First, there must be a blood victim for the undergods.   1255

THEOCLYMENUS

What beast? Only tell me, and I will do your will.

MENELAUS

Decide yourself. Whatever you give will satisfy.

THEOCLYMENUS

Among us barbarians, it would be a bull or horse.

MENELAUS

Give such then, only give nothing which is malformed.

THEOCLYMENUS

Our herds are rich. We have no lack of good victims.   1260

MENELAUS

Coverings are given too for the body, though none is there.

THEOCLYMENUS
That will be done. Is anything else customary?

MENELAUS
Brazen armor; for Menelaus loved the spear . . .

THEOCLYMENUS
What we shall give will be worthy of Pelops' clan.

MENELAUS
. . . and we need too other fair produce of the earth.   1265

THEOCLYMENUS
What will you do? How will you sink all this in the sea?

MENELAUS
A ship must be there, also rowers to man the oars.

THEOCLYMENUS
How far distant is the ship to be from the land?

MENELAUS
Out where the breakers can barely be seen on shore.

THEOCLYMENUS
Tell me, why does Greece have this custom? For what cause?   1270

MENELAUS
So the waves cannot wash pollution back ashore.

THEOCLYMENUS
You shall have a fast-running Phoenician ship, with oars.

MENELAUS
That would be excellent. Menelaus would like it so.

THEOCLYMENUS
Do you need her too? Can you not do it by yourself?

MENELAUS
A man's mother must do this, or his wife, or children.   1275

THEOCLYMENUS
You mean it is her duty to bury her husband?

MENELAUS

It is duty's part not to rob the dead of their due.

THEOCLYMENUS

She may go. A wife kept dutiful is to my own
advantage. Go in, and bring the funeral robes of state.°
And if you act so as to please her, I shall send   1280
you from my country with no empty hands, to bear
a good report of me; you shall have clothing, not
this ragged state, and food, enough to bring you home
again; for now I see you are in hard case.

And you, my dear, do not wear yourself away in longing   1285
for the impossible.° Menelaus has met his fate,
and your dead husband shall not come to life again.

MENELAUS

You see your task, young woman; it is to love and serve
the husband you have, and let the other husband go.
In the circumstances, this is the best that you can do.   1290
But if I come through safe to Hellas, I shall put
an end to former scandals that were said of you.
Only be now the wife that you were meant to be.

HELEN

It shall be so. My husband shall have no complaint
of me. You will be there, and you will know the truth.   1295
Come in the house, poor wanderer, you shall have your bath
and a change of clothing. Kindnesses I have for you
shall not be put off. If I give all you should have
from me, in all the better spirit you will do
the things my dearest Menelaus has deserved.   1300

(Exit Helen, Menelaus, and Theoclymenus into the palace.)

CHORUS [singing]

STROPHE A

Long ago, the Mountain Mother
of all the gods, on flashing feet,

ran down the wooded clefts
of the hills, crossed stream-waters in spate
and the sea's thunderous surf beat   1305
in wild desire for the lost girl
not to be named, her daughter,
and the cry of her voice keened high to break
through mutter of drums and rattles.
And as the goddess harnessed   1310
wild beasts to draw her chariot
in search of the daughter torn away
from the circling pattern of dance where she
and her maidens moved, storm-footed beside°
the mother, Artemis with her bow,   1315
stark-eyed, spear-handed Athena
attended. But Zeus, from his high place
in the upper sky shining° ordained
a different course to follow.

For when the wandering and the swift
course of the mother was done, the far,   1320
the toilsome, the vain search
for her daughter's treacherous capture,
she crossed the place where the mountain nymphs
keep watch in the snows of Ida,
and there cast the blight of her grief   1325
across the stone and snow of the hill forests.°
Earth, green gone from her fields, would give
food no more in the sown lands,
and generations were wasted.
For the flocks she sent out no longer   1330
tender food from the curling leaves.
The cities of men were starving,
the sacrifice to the gods was gone,
no offerings flamed on the altars. She,
turned cruel by grief for her daughter, dried   1335

the springs that gush from deep in the ground,
and there were no jets of bright water.

STROPHE B

But then, as those festivals the gods
share with the race of men died out,
Zeus spoke, to soften the ruinous
rages of the Great Mother: 1340
"Go, stately Graces, and go
Muses, to Deo angered
thus for the sake of the maiden.
Change with wild singing the strain of grief°
in her, and, Muses, you too with hymns and dancing." 1345
It was then that the loveliest
of the immortals took the chthonian
voice of bronze and the skin-strung drums:
Aphrodite. The goddess smiled
and drew into her hands 1350
the deep-sounding pipe
in delight with its music.

ANTISTROPHE B

You had no right in this. The flames you lit°
in your chambers were without sanction.
You showed, child, no due reverence 1355
for this goddess' sacrifice.
You won the Great Mother's anger.
The dappled dress in the deer skin
is a great matter, and the ivy wound
green on the sacred hollow reed 1360
has power; so also the shaken,
the high, the whirled course of the bull-roarer
in the air; so also the dances,
the wild hair shaken for Bromius,
the goddess' nightlong vigils. 1365
It is well that by daylight°

the moon obscures her.
All your claim was your beauty.

(Enter Helen from the palace.)

HELEN

Friends, all that happened in the house was favorable.
The daughter of Proteus keeps our secret. Though she knows   1370
my husband is here, and though her brother questioned her,
she told him nothing, rather she told him he was dead
and buried, out of the sunlight. She did this for me.
My lord has gained a capture, fair and fortunate.°
He took the armor that is to be sunken in the sea   1375
and fitted the shield handle upon his powerful arm
and wears it so, with the spear held in his right hand,
as if working to help grace the dead man. Yet still
first he practiced, with the armor on him, for a fight
as one who would raise a monument over a whole world   1380
of barbarians once we embark in the oared boat;
then I took off the wreck-stained clothes he wore, and gave
him new, and made him fine again, and bathed his body
at last in fresh water drawn from the stream.
                                  But see,   1385
this prince, who now thinks that he has a marriage with me
in his hands' reach, is coming from the house. So I
must talk no longer. We want you on our side.° Control
your lips, be kind, and some day, if we ever save
ourselves from here, we shall attempt to save you too.

(Enter Theoclymenus from the palace, followed by Menelaus, and
accompanied by servants who carry the funeral properties.)

THEOCLYMENUS

Men, go on to your work as the stranger told you to   1390
and take with you the funeral offerings to the sea.
Helen, if what I say to you does not seem wrong,
stay here, as I ask you. Your duty to your husband, whether

you go, or stay, will have been done in any case.
I am afraid longing for him will seize you, make   1395
you fling your body down into the tossing sea
stunned with delights remembered from him before. I know
how much, too much, you mourned for him when he was
   not here.

HELEN

O my new husband, how can I help holding dear
the memory of my first marriage, all the love   1400
and closeness of it? I have loved him well enough
to die when he died. But what grace would he have known
in death from my death? Only let me go, myself
in person, and give his dead body what it deserves.
So may the gods grant you what I would wish to have   1405
them grant you, and this stranger, who is helping here.
For your kindness now to Menelaus and to me
you shall have me in your house, as wife, to the degree
that you deserve, since all this is in fortune's gift.
Now give your orders to the man who will provide   1410
the ship for our conveyance. This will make me happy.

THEOCLYMENUS   (To a servant.)
Go then, get ready a Sidonian fifty-oar
galley; have master rowers aboard; give it to her.

HELEN

Is not this man to be in charge of the funeral ship?

THEOCLYMENUS

Certainly. My sailors are hereby ordered to obey him.   1415

HELEN

Give the order again so they will hear quite clearly.

THEOCLYMENUS

Again, and still a third time, if you wish me to.

HELEN

For your good, and for my good in the things I plan.

THEOCLYMENUS
Now, do not waste yourself with too much weeping.

HELEN
                                    No.
Today will demonstrate my gratitude to you.   1420

THEOCLYMENUS
Remember, the dead are nothing. This is wasted work.

HELEN
It is matters there of which I speak; and matters here.°

THEOCLYMENUS
You will find me as good a man as Menelaus.

HELEN
I ask no more. I need only the favor of fortune.

THEOCLYMENUS
That is in your power, as long as you are kind to me.   1425

HELEN
I don't need teaching now to love those I ought to love.

THEOCLYMENUS
Shall I go too and see the expedition along?

HELEN
Oh no. My lord, you must not do slave's work for your slaves.

THEOCLYMENUS
Very well. I won't do the rituals of the Pelopidae.
My house needs no lustration, since it was not here   1430
that Menelaus died. Therefore, one of you go
and tell my vassals to take the wedding images
inside my palace. All my country must be loud
with singing of congratulation and with strains
of marriage for Helen and me, to bless our state.   1435

                              (Exit a servant to the side.)

Go now, my stranger guest, and give all this to the arms
of the sea, in honor of him who was her husband once,
then make haste back to my house again, and bring my wife,
so that you may be my guest at our wedding feast,
and then go home—or stay and prosper here with me.   1440

(Exit into the palace.)

MENELAUS

O Zeus, renowned as father and wise among the gods,
look down upon us. Grant us surcease from our pain,
and as we grate the shoal-rocks of catastrophe
reach us your hand, touch only with your fingertips—
and we are there, triumphant, where we wish to be.   1445
Our past has been our share of troubles, all our share.
I have said, O gods, much bad of you. I have said good,°
and bad things also. I do not deserve bad luck
forever, but to walk with upright stride. Grant me
this one grace. It will make me happy all my life.   1450

(Helen and Menelaus exit to the side.)

CHORUS [singing]

STROPHE A

Phoenician ship out of Sidon, O°
oars dear to Nereus' splashing water,
after whose lead in the lovely dance
the dolphins skip, when the open sea   1455
sleeps in windless quiet: and she,
Galaneia, who is called Lady of Calms,
and the Great Sea's green-eyed daughter,
so speaks: "You'll set wide the sails on the masts,
leave them free to the salt airs,   1460
but now take in your hands the pinewood oars,
mariners, oh mariners,
as you convey Helen home
to kind haven upon the shores of Perseus."

So, Helen, might you find again   1465
the Daughters of Leucippus there by the river,
or before the temple of Pallas
come back at last to the dances
or the revels for Hyacinthus
and the night-long festival   1470
established by Phoebus after
his whirled throw of the discus°
in games killed him: for the Laconian land
a day of sacrifices
by ordinance of him, son of Zeus;   1475
come back to the girl you left
in your house, Hermione,
for whose marriage the pine flares have not shone yet.

Oh, that we might fly in the air
winged high over Libya
where the lines of the migrant   1480
birds, escaping the winter rain,
take their way, following
the authority of their leader's
whistle. And he flying into the rainless, the wheat-burdened flat   1485
places, screams his clear call.
O flying birds with the long throats, who
share the course of the racing clouds,
go to the midmost Pleiades.
Go to Orion of the night,   1490
cry like heralds your message
as you light down on Eurotas,
that Menelaus has taken the town
of Dardanus and will come home.

May you riding down through the bright   1495
air, swift on your horses,

sons of Tyndareus, come
down the stormy courses of your stars' flaring,
oh, dwellers in the sky,
saviors of Helen, come   1500
cross close on the green swell and the dark-skinned back of the
    rollers
and the gray splash of the breaking sea,
bringing from Zeus those winds that blow
sweet airs for the mariners: 1505
and cast away from your sister the shame
spoken of her barbarian loves,
shame that was hers for punishment
out of the quarrel on Ida, though
she never went to the land of Troy,   1510
not to the towers of Phoebus.

                    (Enter Servant of Theoclymenus from the side.)

SERVANT

My lord, the worst of news from our house. We have just
    learned.°

                    (Enter Theoclymenus from the palace.)

Fresh news, strange news and bad. Hear it from me at once.

THEOCLYMENUS
    What is it?

SERVANT
    Your work is wasted for a wife who is not
    yours. Helen is gone away, out of our land.   1515

THEOCLYMENUS
    How gone? On wings, or do her feet still tread the earth?

SERVANT
    Menelaus carried her away. For that was he.
    He came himself, and brought the news of his own death.

THEOCLYMENUS

    This is disgraceful. But still I cannot quite believe.

    What sort of transport carried them away from here?   1520

SERVANT

    Precisely what you gave your guest. He took your men

    and left you. There you have it in a single word.

THEOCLYMENUS

    How? I must understand this, and I cannot yet

    credit it that a single arm could overpower

    so many sailors, all those who were sent with you.   1525

SERVANT

    After Zeus' daughter left the palace here and you,

    and was escorted to the sea, there as she placed

    her tiny feet, she mourned aloud, most cleverly,

    for that husband who was by her side, by no means dead.

    Now as we came to your shipyards and your arsenal

    we hauled down a Sidonian ship of the first class   1530

    with fifty rowing benches to accommodate

    the oars. And now our various duties were assigned.

    One man set up the mast, another set the oars

    in place, while yet another had charge of the white sails,°   1535

    the steersman sat to the tiller and the steering gear.

    Now as we were hard at it, there came down to the shore

    certain Greek men who had sailed with Menelaus once

    and who had been watching for just this. They wore the rags

    of shipwreck. Fine-looking men, but in a filthy state.   1540

    The son of Atreus saw them as they came, and made

    a false pretense of pity for our benefit,

    with: "Poor castaways, what ship? It must once have been

    Achaean, cracked up now, and so we see you here.

    Will you help bury Atreus' fallen son? His wife,   1545

    Tyndareus' daughter, buries him in effigy.

    This is she." They then let fall some fictitious tears

    and took aboard what was to be sunk in the depths

for Menelaus. We had our suspicions here,
and there were words among us, how these newcomers   1550
were very numerous. Nevertheless we held our peace.
We had orders from you and kept them. You had said
your guest was to have full command. That ruined all.
Now all the cargo was light and easily picked up
and stowed inside the ship, except the bull, who stood   1555
and balked at going up on the steep-slanted plank,
but bellowed aloud, and with arched back and head low down
rolled his eyes round the circle past his lowered horns
forbidding all to touch him. Helen's husband raised
his voice, and cried: "Oh, you who captured Ilium,   1560
come, do it the Greek way, can you not? Hoist the bull's
weight on the strength of your young shoulders, heave him in
over the prow." And saying this he raised his sword.°
"For he shall be our sacrifice to the dead man."
They at his order went and laid hands on the bull   1565
and heaved him up and forced him on the rowing deck.
And Menelaus rubbed the horse's neck and forehead,
persuading him, without harness, to go inside the ship.

At last, when all was got aboard and stowed away,
Helen, with dainty steps, put her feet through the rungs   1570
of the ladder, and took possession of the central bench,
with Menelaus, the supposed dead man, by her side,
and left and right along the bulkheads all took place,
man ranked on man in order (but the Greeks had swords
hidden away beneath their garments).
                                        Then we all   1575
whitened the water at the bosun's shout of "Row!"
Now when we had reached a point where we were not remote
from the land, nor near it either, then our steersman asked:
"Shall we make further out, my friend, or is this far
enough to suit you? What we do is yours to say."   1580
He said: "This will do." Then, with a sword in his right hand,
crept to the prow, and braced himself to strike the bull,

and where he stood, there were no dead men in his mind,
but as he cut the throat he prayed: "Lord of the sea,
Poseidon in the depth, and you, chaste Nereids,   1585
convey me safe to Nauplia's strand, convey my wife
who left it, but was chaste." And as he spoke, the blood
rained on the water, favoring the stranger's prayer.
One of us said then: "There is treacherous sailing here.
We must make back. You, give the order for right oar,   1590
and you, reverse the rudder." But now Atreus' son
stood from the slaughtered ox and hailed his company:
"Oh, flower of all the land of Greece, why longer wait
to smash these barbarians, cut them down and throw them
      off
the ship into the water." Then your bosun called   1595
aloud upon your seamen to resist: "Come on!
Get anything to fight with. Take the end of a spar;
break up a bench and use it, or an unshipped oar,
and smash the heads of these foreigners, who turned on us."
Both sides sprang to their feet then. We laid hands upon   1600
whatever ship's lumber we could find. But they had swords.
The ship ran blood; but there was Helen cheering them
on from the stern: "Where is the glory of Troy? Come on,
show it on these barbarians." Then all fought hard,
and some went down, some kept their feet, but a man down   1605
was a man dead. Menelaus had his armor on
and watched where his companions had the worst of it
and there rallied them, with his sword in his right hand,
so that men, to escape, dived overboard. He swept
the rowing benches clean of your mariners, then went   1610
to the rudder and made the helmsman steer the ship for
      Greece,
and they got the mast up, and a wind came, favoring them.

They are gone from your country. I myself, escaping death,
let myself into the water where the anchor hung,
and as I was failing, one of the fishermen at his lines   1615

pulled me out and set me ashore so I could bring
this message to you. Man's most valuable trait
is a judicious sense of what not to believe.

(Exit to the side.)

CHORUS LEADER

I never would have thought Menelaus could be here
unknown, my lord, to you and us. Yet so it was.   1620

*(As Theoclymenus speaks the next lines, he starts
to rush into the palace, but his way is blocked by
another Servant, an attendant of Theonoë.)*

THEOCLYMENUS

Oh, I have been duped and tricked with women's artful
   treacheries.
Now my bride has escaped away, and if they could be
   overtaken
I would make all haste to catch the ship that carries those
   foreigners.
But at least I can take vengeance on the sister who betrayed
me, who saw Menelaus in my house and did not tell me so.   1625
She shall never again deceive anyone with her prophecies.

SERVANT

Hallo, you there, master, where are you going? Is it death you
   mean?

THEOCLYMENUS

I am going where justice takes me. Out of my way and stand
   aside.

SERVANT

It is a monstrous thing to rush to. I will not let go my hold.

THEOCLYMENUS

You, a slave, will overpower your master?

SERVANT

                              Yes. I have good sense.   1630

THEOCLYMENUS

No good to me, unless you let me go . . .

SERVANT

But that I will not do.

THEOCLYMENUS

. . . and kill my hateful sister . . .

SERVANT

No, not hateful. Dutiful.

THEOCLYMENUS

. . . who betrayed me . . .

SERVANT

A noble betrayal. What she did was right.

THEOCLYMENUS

. . . giving my bride away to others.

SERVANT

Others had more right than you.

THEOCLYMENUS

Who has right over what is mine?

SERVANT

The man her father gave her to.   1635

THEOCLYMENUS

Fortune gave her then to me.

SERVANT

And fate took her away again.

THEOCLYMENUS

You are not to judge what I do.

SERVANT

If I am in the right, I must.

THEOCLYMENUS

Then I am no longer ruler, but am ruled.

SERVANT

For right, not wrong.

THEOCLYMENUS

You desire to die, I think.

SERVANT

Then kill me, but you shall not kill
your sister while I have the power to stop you. Slaves, if they
    are true,   1640
find no glory greater than to perish for their masters' sake.

(Enter Castor and Polydeuces above the palace.)

CASTOR

Lord of this land, Theoclymenus, restrain the rage
that carries you off your true course. We are the twins
called Dioscuri, sons of Zeus, whom Leda once
gave birth to, with that Helen who has fled your house.   1645
That marriage over which you rage was not to be,
nor has the daughter of the divine Nereid done
you wrong, Theonoë your sister, but she kept
the righteous orders of her father and the gods.
It had always been ordained that for the present time°   1650
Helen was to be a dweller in your house. But when
Troy was uptorn from its foundations, and she lent
the gods her name for it, this was no more to be,
for now she must be once more married with her own,
and go home, and live with her husband. Therefore, hold   1655
your hand, nor darken your sword with a sister's blood.
Believe it was in thoughtful care that she did this.
We would have saved our sister long ago, since Zeus
had made us into gods and we had power, except
that we were weaker still than destiny, and less   1660
than the other gods, whose will was that these things
    should be.

This is for you. Henceforward, let my sister hear:
sail with your husband, sail on. You shall have fair wind.

We, your twin brothers, guardian divinities,
shall ride the open water and bring you safely home.   1665
And when your life turns its last course and makes an end,
you shall be called, with the two sons of Zeus, divine,
have your libations,° and with us be venerated
as honored guests by mortals. Zeus has willed it so.
And where the son of Maia first defined your place   1670
when he caught you up from Sparta on the skyward way,
stealing you so that Paris might not have you, where
the island stretches to guard Acte, shall its name
be known as "Helen," meaning "Captive," for mankind
hereafter; because you were stolen from your house.   1675
For Menelaus, who has wandered much, the gods
have granted a home upon the Island of the Blest.
For Heaven never hates the noble in the end,
though their lives are often harder than the nameless
　　multitude's.°

THEOCLYMENUS

O sons of Leda and of Zeus, I will forego   1680
the quarrel I used to have for your sister's sake.
Nor do I wish to kill my sister now. Then let°
Helen go home, if so the gods would have it. Know
that you are born of the same blood from which was born
the best and the most faithful sister in the world.°   1685
Go then rejoicing for the great and noble heart
in her. There are not many women such as she.

　　　　　　　(*Exit with Servant into the palace. Exit the Dioscuri.*)

CHORUS [*chanting*]
Many are the forms of what is unknown.°
Much that the gods achieve is surprise.
What we look for does not come to pass;   1690
a god finds a way for what none foresaw.
Such was the end of this story.

THE PHOENICIAN
WOMEN

Translated by ELIZABETH WYCKOFF

THE PHOENICIAN WOMEN: INTRODUCTION

The Play: Date and Composition

It is not certain when Euripides' *Phoenician Women* was first produced, but external evidence, supported by metrical features, suggests a date of around 411-409. Presumably Euripides wrote it for the annual competition at the Great Dionysian Festival in Athens. What the other three plays were in Euripides' tetralogy of that year is unknown; a very poorly preserved "hypothesis" (ancient scholarly summary) preceding the play in a number of manuscripts perhaps indicates that he came in second in that competition.

Ancient scholars noted that the play has an abundance of scenes of suffering, that it presents many characters, and that it is full of finely phrased maxims. They stated their approval of the theatricality of its visual spectacle but criticized it for containing a number of irrelevant scenes: in particular, Antigone's view of the enemy captains from the walls of the city, Polynices' arrival in Thebes under truce to negotiate with his brother, and Oedipus' lyric song and banishment at the end of the play. Many modern scholars too have been bothered by what they have considered to be the play's excessive length, repetitiousness, contradictions, and extraneous material, as well as by numerous smaller metrical and linguistic difficulties, and have suggested that the text as we have it contains a number of interpolations, including not only isolated lines and groups of lines but even entire scenes. Suspicion has fallen especially upon Antigone's view from the walls, Eteocles' farewell speech, the Messenger's catalogue of the seven champions, Creon's lament for his dead son, and the ending of the play; and it has been suggested that some or all of these pas-

sages may have been composed by other poets for later perfor-
mances. But recent critics have been more cautious about con-
demning whole sections of the tragedy as inauthentic; some have
pointed out that the play as a whole is a kind of encyclopedic
compendium of motifs and topics from the Theban mythic complex and that overfullness and the inclusion of only tangentially
related material are part of its very character. The question remains open.

The Myth

The play's title does not provide much of a clue regarding its
mythic content. Instead it designates the chorus, which is composed of Phoenician women from the city of Tyre who have been
sent to Delphi to serve Apollo in his temple but, having stopped
on the way in Thebes, are unexpectedly trapped there by the Argive invasion. Their relation to the events of the play is thus little
more than that of horrified witnesses—though they are also connected to what happens in Thebes by a very remote genealogical
link: Cadmus, the founder of Thebes, was originally from Tyre
too.

The Phoenician Women dramatizes the attack of the Seven
against Thebes, one of the grimmest episodes from a legendary saga that was very popular and well known to Euripides' audience: the vicissitudes of the Labdacids, the royal dynasty of
Thebes—King Laius, his wife Jocasta, and their son Oedipus, and
then the children of Oedipus and Jocasta's incestuous marriage,
Eteocles, Polynices, Antigone, and Ismene. The story had been an
important part of early Greek epic and had continued to remain
a familiar theme of lyric poetry (most notably in Stesichorus, a
poet of the sixth century BCE), oral legend, and tragedy. While the
different versions often varied significantly in outcome, charac-
terization, motivation, and moral evaluation, the basic outline remained constant from version to version. After Oedipus' removal
from the throne, his sons Eteocles and Polynices could not share
the rule of Thebes amicably. They arranged to alternate annually

as sole ruler, but when Polynices' time came Eteocles refused to yield the kingship and instead exiled him to Argos. There Polynices raised an army that he and six other champions led to attack seven-gated Thebes. The Argive invaders were defeated and their champions were slain—Eteocles and Polynices killed each other. Creon, the new ruler of Thebes, adopted the extreme measure of refusing to grant Polynices burial.

The myth was one of the most frequently dramatized in Attic tragedy. Most of the other tragic versions seem, as far as we can tell, to have focused on only one episode of the story in any one play. Thus the account of three generations of the Labdacids had been presented by Aeschylus in the three plays of a connected trilogy (468 BCE): the first two plays, *Laius* and *Oedipus*, have been lost, but the third one, *The Seven against Thebes*, recounting the attack of the Seven, survives (ancient scholars noted that *The Phoenician Women* presents the same mythic material as does this play but adds Jocasta). Sophocles at different points in his career devoted at least three plays, all of which survive, to individual tragic events from this mythic complex: *Antigone* (ca. 440 BCE), on the aftermath of the attack of the Seven and Antigone's decision to bury Polynices despite Creon's prohibition; *Oedipus the King* (date unknown), on Oedipus' discovery that he is the killer of his father and the husband of his mother; and *Oedipus at Colonus* (406 BCE), on his reception as a refugee and eventual death in the local district of Colonus in Attica.

Among Euripides' other surviving tragedies, only his *Suppliant Women* (produced about 423 BCE), which presents the aftermath of the defeat of the Seven, derives from this complex of Theban legends. Euripides is also known to have written at least two lost plays on the subject: *Chrysippus*, on the origin of the gods' hatred for Laius, and *Oedipus*, in which Oedipus is blinded by Laius' servants before his identity is revealed. He also wrote an *Antigone* (also lost), about which very little is known.

In contrast to the apparent tendency of the other tragedians, Euripides' *Phoenician Women* presents a comprehensive synopsis of the whole story by focusing one after another on a large variety of events, characters, and themes all having to do with the fall of Oedipus' family. The play begins with a monologue by Oedipus' wife and mother, Jocasta, mother of the two brothers Eteocles and Polynices. (In this version, unlike in Sophocles' *Oedipus the King*, she has not committed suicide upon discovering that Oedipus is her son.) Then Antigone appears on the top of the palace together with her old tutor; in a scene reminiscent of Aeschylus' *Seven against Thebes*, the tutor identifies for her the seven enemy captains who will attack the city. Polynices enters to negotiate, futilely, with Eteocles. In this play, in what is presumably a surprising Euripidean innovation, Polynices is the more positive character. Then Teiresias announces that Thebes can be saved only if Creon's son Menoeceus is sacrificed; Creon refuses, but Menoeceus tricks him and goes off to commit suicide. The Thebans defeat the enemy army but the two brothers kill each other and Jocasta slays herself on their corpses. Antigone is left to mourn the three corpses together with old Oedipus, who in a final dramatic surprise enters from the palace to witness and lament the end of his lineage.

Transmission and Reception

The evidence of quotations and allusions among later authors and the survival of at least twenty-four papyri and other ancient texts containing fragments of the play (more than for any other Greek tragedy except Euripides' *Orestes*) indicate that *The Phoenician Women* was extremely popular throughout antiquity, perhaps in part because it provides a kind of handy compendium of the legends relating to the house of the Labdacids. Further evidence for the play's continuing vitality on ancient stages may be the numerous interpolations in the text that have been detected by scholars; some of these may well have been due to expansion by directors or actors. *The Phoenician Women* not only was selected as one of the ten canonical plays of Euripides most studied and read in antiquity, but, together with *Hecuba* and *Orestes*, became one of the three plays of the so-called Byzantine triad. As a result, it is transmitted by hundreds of medieval manuscripts and is equipped with very full ancient and medieval commentaries. Given the great popularity of Euripides in later antiquity, and of *The Phoenician Women* in particular, it was inevitable that Greek and Latin authors who portrayed the fall of the Labdacids drew upon this tragedy even more than upon Aeschylus' *Seven against Thebes* or Sophocles' *Antigone*. Thus it was on Euripides' play that Seneca based his own (incomplete) tragedy *Phoenician Women* and Statius his epic poem *Thebaid*, which transmitted the story to the Latin Middle Ages.

The popularity of *The Phoenician Women* (and of Statius' *Thebaid*) in the Middle Ages meant that during the Renaissance in the West this continued to be one of the most widely read tragedies. It inspired such dramatists as Jean Racine (*La Thébaïde*, 1664) and Vittorio Alfieri (*Polinice*, 1783) and was translated by Hugo Grotius (1630) and Friedrich Schiller (1789). But by the end of the eighteenth century its fortunes had already begun to decline. Precisely its combination of extreme pathos and polished rhetoric and the fullness of its treatment of the legend, which had helped secure its success in earlier ages, made it inimical to the taste of the Romantics and later writers; and the increasing popularity of Aeschylus and especially of Sophocles meant that, in the past two centuries, their versions have eclipsed Euripides'. A production by the Royal Shakespeare Company, directed by Katie Mitchell in 1995, is one of the few professional stagings of the play in the modern era. Perhaps now, with changes in our world and in our tastes, the time is right for its revival.

THE PHOENICIAN WOMEN

Characters   JOCASTA, mother and wife of Oedipus; sister of
Creon
OLD TUTOR
ANTIGONE, daughter of Oedipus and Jocasta;
sister of Polynices and Eteocles
CHORUS of young women from Phoenicia
POLYNICES, son of Oedipus and Jocasta; brother
of Eteocles and Antigone
ETEOCLES, son of Oedipus and Jocasta; brother
of Polynices and Antigone
CREON, brother of Jocasta
TEIRESIAS, a blind Theban seer
MENOECEUS, son of Creon
TWO MESSENGERS
OEDIPUS, husband of Jocasta; father of
Antigone, Polynices, and Eteocles

Scene: Thebes, before the royal palace. Jocasta enters from its door.

JOCASTA
You who cut your way through heaven's stars,°
riding the chariot with its welded gold,
Sun, with your swift mares whirling forth your light,
evil the shaft you sent to Thebes that day
when Cadmus came here, leaving Phoenicia's shore,   5
he who wed Cypris' child, Harmonia,

fathering Polydorus, who in turn
had Labdacus, they say, and he had Laius.

      Now I am known as daughter of Menoeceus,   10
Creon my brother by the selfsame mother,°
my name Jocasta, as my father gave it,
Laius my husband. When he still was childless
after long marriage with me in the palace,
he went to Phoebus asking and beseeching   15
that we might share male children for the house.
But he said, "Lord of Thebes and its famed horses,
sow not that furrow against divine decree.
For if you have a child, him you beget
shall kill you, and your house shall wade through blood."   20
But Laius, in his lust, and drunk beside,
begot a child on me, yet when he had,
knowing his error, as the god had said it,
he gave the child to shepherds to expose
in Hera's Field, high on Cithaeron's rock,   25
when he had pinned its ankles with sharp iron°
(and this is why Greece called him Oedipus).
Then Polybus' herdsman took the child
and brought it home and gave it to their mistress.
She took my labor's fruit and, nursing it,   30
convinced her husband to rear it as her own.

      When his red beard was growing, my young son,
who had guessed or heard the truth, set off to learn,
at Phoebus' shrine, his parents. So did Laius,   35
seeking to learn if the child he had exposed
were still alive. They met in middle journey
at the same spot in the split road of Phocis.
Then Laius' driver ordered him away:
"Stranger, yield place to princes." But he went on,   40
silent, in pride. So with their sharp-edged hooves
the mares of Laius bloodied up his feet.
And so—why give the details of disaster?—
a son slew his father, and he took the team

to give to Polybus, his foster parent.
When the Sphinx attacked and crushed our city down,   45
my husband gone, Creon proclaimed my marriage:
whoever might solve the clever maiden's riddle,
to him I should be wed. And so it happened.
Oedipus, my son, did somehow guess her song.   50
So he became the ruler of this land°
and got the scepter of this realm as prize.
Poor man, unknowing, he wedded with his mother;
nor did she know she bedded with her son.

      And to my son I bore two further sons,   55
Eteocles and famous Polynices,
and daughters two. Her father named Ismene
while I before had named Antigone.
When Oedipus learned I was his wife and mother,
he who'd endured all suffering then struck   60
with terrible gory wounding his own eyes,
bleeding the pupils with a golden brooch.
When his sons' beards had grown, they shut him up
behind the bolts, that this fate might be forgotten—
though it needed much contrivance to conceal.   65
There in the house he lives, and struck by fate
he has called unholy curses on his children:
that they'll divide this house with sharpened steel.

      They were afraid that if they lived together   70
the gods might grant his prayers. So they agreed
that Polynices should go, a willing exile,
while Eteocles stayed in this land and held the scepter,
to change though, year by year. Yet when Eteocles
sat safe on high, he would not leave the throne,
but kept his brother exiled from this land.   75
He went to Argos, married Adrastus' daughter,
and brought the Argive force he had collected
against these very seven-gated walls,
seeking his share of the land, and his father's scepter.   80
I have persuaded son to come to son

under a truce before they take to arms.
I hope for peace. The messenger says he'll come.
　　　O Zeus who lives in heaven's shining folds
save us and let my sons be reconciled.   85
If you are wise you should not leave a mortal
constantly wretched throughout his whole life.

(Exit Jocasta into the palace. Antigone and
the old Tutor appear on its roof.)

TUTOR
Antigone, flower of your father's house,
your mother has said you may leave the maiden's room
to climb the very steepest of the roof   90
and see the Argive army, as you asked.
But wait, that I may track the road before you
in case some citizen is in the way.
If so, some blame would come on me the slave,   95
and on your highness. Since I know, I'll tell
all that I saw and heard among the Argives
when I went there from here to make the truce
with your brother, and also when I came back again.
　　　No citizen is near the house at all.
Try the old cedar ladder with your feet,   100
look over the plain and see by Ismenus' stream
and Dirce's spring how great the enemy host.

(Antigone goes up to the top of the steps.)

ANTIGONE [*singing, and then alternately singing and speaking in this*
lyric interchange while the Tutor speaks in response]
　　Reach your old hand to my young one. Help me step
　　up from the stairs.   105

TUTOR
Take hold, my girl. You're here, but just in time.
The Argive army is moving, the companies part.

ANTIGONE

Hecate, Leto's child! The lightning-shine   110
of bronze all over the plain!

TUTOR

Polynices comes no trifler to this land.
He brings the clamor of many horse and foot.

ANTIGONE

The gates, and their locks! Are the brazen bolts
holding firm Amphion's wall of stone?   115

TUTOR

Take heart, all's well and safe inside the city.°
Look at the first man, if you want to mark him.

ANTIGONE

Who is he with the crest of white
who comes at the head of the host and lightly shakes   120
the brazen shield on his arm?

TUTOR

A captain, lady.°

ANTIGONE

                Yes, but who, and whence?
[*speaking*]
Speak out, old man, and tell me: what's his name?

TUTOR

He boasts his birth from Mycenae and he lives   125
by Lerna's waters: lord Hippomedon.

ANTIGONE [*singing*]

How prideful, how hateful to see!
Like an earth-born giant hurling flame in a picture,   130
not like the race of day.

TUTOR

Do you see that captain crossing Dirce's stream?

ANTIGONE [*speaking*]

How strange, how strange his arms! And who is he?°

TUTOR

Tydeus, the warrior from far Aetolia.

ANTIGONE [*singing*]

Is this the one who has married the very sister   135
of Polynices' bride?

[*speaking*]
How strange his arms, half-barbarous to see!

TUTOR

All the Aetolians carry such a shield
and hurl their javelins, child, to hit the mark.   140

ANTIGONE

Old man, how did you learn all this so well?°

TUTOR

I knew them, for I saw their arms before
when I went from here to there to make the truce
with your brother. So I know them in their harness.

ANTIGONE

Who is this one who comes by Zethus' tomb,

[*singing*]
with falling curls,   145
a youth, and frightful to see?

[*speaking*]
Some captain, since an armed crowd follows on.

TUTOR

Parthenopaeus, Atalanta's son.   150

ANTIGONE [*singing*]

I hope that Artemis, ranging the hills, kills his mother
with her shaft and destroys him
who comes to plunder my town.

TUTOR

    I hope so, child. But the right is on their side.
    And I am afraid the gods may see things clearly.   155

ANTIGONE

    And where is he whom my selfsame mother bore
    to a painful fate?

    [*speaking*]
    Dear old man, tell me, where is Polynices?

TUTOR

    He stands with Adrastus, close by the maidens' tomb,
    Niobe's seven daughters. You see him now?   160

ANTIGONE

    Not clearly, but enough to guess his shape.

    [*singing*]
    Oh, could I run on my feet like a wind-swift cloud through the sky
    to my own dear brother, and throw my arms round his neck,   165
    poor exile—but how

    [*speaking*]
    he shines forth in his golden arms, old man,

    [*singing*]
    ablaze with the light of dawn.

TUTOR

    He is coming to this house, you may be glad,   170
    under a truce.

ANTIGONE [*speaking*]

                  But who comes here, old man?
    Who mounts and drives a chariot of white?

TUTOR

    That is the prophet Amphiaraus, lady,
    bringing the victims whose blood shall please this land.

ANTIGONE [*singing*]

    Selene, daughter of shining-girdled Sun,°   175

you with your round gold light, how calm he comes,
how gently guides his horses!

[*speaking*]
Where is the man who insulted us so fiercely,
Capaneus?

TUTOR
                   There he marks the approaches out,   180
takes the walls' measures up and down the towers.

ANTIGONE [*singing*]
Nemesis, and you, deep thunder of Zeus,
and shining flare of the lightning, it is for you
to put his boasting to sleep.
He said he would bring the Theban girls°   185
as slaves to Mycenae's women,
would give them to Lerna's triple fount,
slaves to Poseidon's lover's waters.
Artemis, golden-haired, child of Zeus, may I never   190
endure that slavery!

TUTOR
Child, back into the house, and stay inside
your maiden chamber. You have had the joy
of that desired sight you wished to see.   195
Noise in the city proves a crowd of women
is pressing toward the royal palace now.
The female sex is very quick to blame.
If one of them gets a little launching place,
far, far she drives. There seems to be some pleasure   200
for women in ill talk of one another.

        (*Exit Antigone and the Tutor into the palace. Enter*
        from the side the Chorus of Phoenician women.)

CHORUS [*singing*]
        STROPHE A
I came, I left the wave of Tyre,
the island of Phoenicia,

as prize for Loxias, slave to Phoebus' house,   205
to rest by Parnassus' snowy ridge.
I came on a ship through the Ionians' sea,
over the fruitless plain,   210
though the west wind rushed past Sicily,
a beautiful blast from heaven.

Chosen most beautiful of my town,
an offering to Apollo,   215
I came to Cadmus' land, as I am Agenor's kin,
sent to Laius' kindred towers.
Like the golden statue-girls,   220
I have begun to serve Phoebus.
But Castalia's water is waiting still
to wet my hair for his service.   225

O rock that shines in the fire,
double gleam on the heights
where Dionysus dances,
and vine that distils the daily wealth,   230
the fruitful cluster of grapes,
holy cave of the serpent, mountain rocks
where the goddesses keep watch, O sacred mountain of snow,
may I, unfearing, dance the Immortals' dance   235
by Phoebus' central hollow, with Dirce left behind.

Now before the walls
savage Ares comes   240
kindling the flame of death
for this city—may it not happen.
Shared are the griefs of friends,
shared; if she must suffer,
this seven-gated land, then does Phoenicia share it.   245
Common blood, common children,

through Io who wore the horns.
I share in these troubles.

A cloud about the town,   250
a close cloud of shields,
kindles the scheme of death.
Soon shall Ares know
that he brings to Oedipus' sons
the curse of the very Furies.   255
Ancestral Argos, I fear your strength,
and I fear the gods' part too.
For this man at arms
comes against our home with justice.   260

(Enter from the side Polynices, with drawn sword.)

POLYNICES

The warders' bolts have let me through the walls
with ease, and so I fear once in the net
I won't get out unbloodied. Thus I look   265
hither and yonder, watching for a trick.
My hand that holds this sword will give me courage.
     Ah, who is there? Or is it a noise I fear?
All things seem terrible to those who dare   270
when they set foot upon the enemy's land.
I trust my mother, and I do not trust her,
who brought me here under a pledge of truce.
Defense is close. The sacrificial hearths   275
are near, nor is the palace desolate.
I'll thrust my sword in the darkness of its case
and ask who are these women by the house.
     Say, foreign ladies, what land did you leave
to come to our Greek halls?

CHORUS LEADER

It was Phoenicia reared me. Agenor's grandsons   280
have sent me here a captive, prize for Phoebus.

And while the son of Oedipus delayed
to send me on to Loxias' oracle
there came the Argives' war against this city.   285
Give answer in return, you who have come
to the gated fortress of the Theban land.

POLYNICES
  My father is Oedipus, Laius' son, my mother
  Jocasta, daughter of Menoeceus.
  The Theban people call me Polynices.   290

CHORUS LEADER
  Kin of Agenor's children who are my lords,°
  who sent me here!

CHORUS [*singing*]
  Master, I fall on my knees,
  heeding the habit of home.
  At last you have come to your father's land.   295
  Queen, queen, come forth,
  open the gates!
  Mother who bore him, do you hear us now?
  Why your delay in leaving the halls
  and taking your son in your arms?   300

                            (*Enter Jocasta from the palace.*)

JOCASTA [*singing*]
  I heard your Phoenician cry,°
  girls, and my poor old feet,
  trembling, have brought me out.
  My child, my child, at last I see you again.   305
  Embrace your mother's breast with your arms,
  stretch forth your face and your dark curly hair,
  to shadow my throat.
  Oh, oh, you have finally come,
  unhoped for, unexpected, to your mother's arms.   310
  What shall I say, how phrase the whole

delight in words and actions
that compasses me about? 315
If I dance in my joy shall I find the old delight?
Child, you went as an exile; your father's house
was left in desolation, your brother's doing.
But your own yearned after you, 320
Thebes itself yearned.
And so I weep, and cut my whitened hair.
No longer, child, do I wear white robes,
I have changed to these dark gloomy rags. 325
And the old man in the house, the blind old man,
since the pair of you left the house,
clings to his weeping desire. He seeks the sword 330
for death by his own hand; he casts a noose
over the roof beams mourning his curse on his children.
He is hidden in darkness and steadily wails his woe. 335
But I hear that you have paired yourself in marriage,
the joy of making children.
In a foreign house you have taken a foreign bride, 340
a curse to your mother and Laius who was of old.
Doom brought by your wedding!
I did not light your wedding° torch
as a happy mother should. 345
Ismenus gave no water to the marriage;
the coming of your bride was never sung in Thebes.
May the cause of these sufferings perish, be it the steel 350
or Strife, or your father, or a demon-rout
in Oedipus' house.
For all their grief has fallen upon me.

CHORUS LEADER

How strange and terrible for women is childbirth! 355
Therefore all women love their children so.

POLYNICES

Mother, with reason, unreasoning have I come
among my enemies. But all men must still

love their own country. Who says something else
enjoys his talk while thinking far away.   360
      I was so scared, had gone so far in fear
lest my brother's tricks might kill me on the way,
that through the town I came with sword in hand,
turning my face about. Just one thing helped,   365
the truce—and your own pledge which led me on
through the ancestral walls. I came in tears
seeing at last the halls and the gods' altars,
the schools that reared me, and the spring of Dirce,
from all of which unjustly banished now
I live in a foreign town, eyes blurred with tears.   370
      I come from grief and find you grief indeed.
Your hair is shorn; your garments are of black.
Alas, alas, my sorrows and myself!
Mother, how frightful is the strife of kindred,
and reconciling is hard to bring about!°   375
What does my father do within the house,
he who sees darkness? What of my two sisters,
do they, poor girls, lament my exile now?

JOCASTA [*now speaking*]
Some god is ruining all of Oedipus' children.
The beginning was my bearing a forbidden child.   380
It was wrong to marry your father and bear you.
But what of this? The god's will must be endured.
Still, I must ask you, fearing it may sting,
one question for whose answer I am yearning.

POLYNICES
Ask openly, leave nothing out at all.   385
Your wish is mine, my mother.

JOCASTA
So now I ask what first I wish to know.°
What is it to lose your country—a great suffering?

POLYNICES

The greatest, even worse than people say.

JOCASTA

What is its nature? What's so hard on exiles?   390

POLYNICES

One thing is worst: a man can't speak out freely.

JOCASTA

But this is slavery, not to speak one's thought.

POLYNICES

One must endure the unwisdom of one's masters.

JOCASTA

This also is painful, to join with fools in folly.

POLYNICES

One must be a slave, for gain, against one's nature.   395

JOCASTA

The saying is that exiles feed on hopes.

POLYNICES

Lovely to look at, but they do delay.

JOCASTA

And doesn't time make clear that they are empty?

POLYNICES

They have seductive charm in a man's troubles.

JOCASTA

How were you fed before your marriage fed you?   400

POLYNICES

Sometimes I'd have a day's worth, sometimes not.

JOCASTA

Your father's foreign friends, were they no help?

POLYNICES

Hope to be rich! If you are not—no friends.

JOCASTA

Your high birth brought you to no lordly height?

POLYNICES

Need's the bad thing. My breeding did not feed me.　　　　405

JOCASTA

It seems one's country is the dearest thing.

POLYNICES

You couldn't say in words how dear it is.

JOCASTA

How did you get to Argos, and with what plan?

POLYNICES

Apollo gave Adrastus a certain answer.

JOCASTA

What sort? Why mention this? I cannot guess.　　　　410

POLYNICES

To marry his daughters to a boar and a lion.

JOCASTA

What has my son to do with wild beasts' names?

POLYNICES

I do not know. God called me to my fate.

JOCASTA

For the god is wise. How did you meet your marriage?

POLYNICES

It was night; I came upon Adrastus' portal.　　　　415

JOCASTA

A wandering exile, looking for a bed?

POLYNICES

Just so—and then another exile came.

JOCASTA

And who was he? Wretched as you, no doubt.

POLYNICES

That Tydeus who is named as Oeneus' son.

JOCASTA

But why did Adrastus think you were those beasts?   420

POLYNICES

Because we fought over the pallet there.

JOCASTA

And then he understood the oracle?

POLYNICES

And gave us two his daughters two to wed.

JOCASTA

Were you happy or unhappy in these weddings?

POLYNICES

Right to this day I have no fault to find.   425

JOCASTA

How did you get the army to follow you here?

POLYNICES

Adrastus promised his two sons-in-law,
Tydeus and me—Tydeus is now my kinsman—°
that both would be brought home, but I the first.
So many Mycenaean chiefs are here   430
and many Danaans, doing me a favor
which hurts me, though I need it. My own town
I fight against. I call the gods to witness:
against my will I fight my willing kindred.
But you can possibly undo these troubles.   435

Mother, you reconcile these kindred-friends,°
save you and me and the city from these sorrows.
This has been sung before, but I shall say it:°
"Men honor property above all else;
it has the greatest power in human life."   440
And so I seek it with ten thousand spears.
A beggar is no nobleman at all.

(Enter Eteocles from the side.)

CHORUS LEADER
Here comes Eteocles to hold his parley.
Jocasta, as their mother, it's for you
to say the words to reconcile your sons.   445

ETEOCLES
Mother, I'm here. I came to do a favor
for you. Now what's to come? Let someone speak.
I have broken off my marshalling of warriors°
about the walls that I might hear from you
at your persuasion the arbitration for which   450
you admitted this man within the city walls.

JOCASTA
Wait for a moment. Swiftness brings not justice.
It is slow speech that brings the greatest wisdom.
Check your dread glare, the seethings of your spirit.
It is not Gorgon's severed head you see;   455
you look upon your brother who has come.
And you, Polynices, look upon your brother,
for if you look upon his face once more
you will speak better and will hear him better.
    I want to give you both some good advice.   460
When friend falls out with friend and they come together
looking at one another, let them look
at that for which they came, forget old wrongs.
Son, Polynices, you may speak the first.   465

For you have come, and brought the Argive army,
as one who claims a wrong. Now may some god
be judge and reconciler of these griefs.

POLYNICES

The word of truth is single in its nature;
and a just cause needs no interpreting.   470
It carries its own case. But the unjust argument,
since it is sick, needs clever medicine.
        I took good foresight for our father's house,
for him, and for myself, hoping to flee
those curses with which once our father cursed us.   475
So willingly myself I left this land,
leaving the rule to him for a year's circle,
so that I myself might take the rule in turn.°
Thus we would not fall into hate and envy
doing and suffering evil—but that has happened.   480
For he who swore this, and called the gods to witness,
did nothing of what he promised and still holds
the kingship and his share of my own house.
        And now I am ready, if I get my own,
to send away the army from this land,   485
to take my own house for my proper turn,
and yield it back to him for equal time,
so as not to plunder my country nor besiege
her towers with the scaling ladder's steps.
But if I get not justice I shall try   490
to do exactly this. The gods be witness:
I have done all in justice, but most unjustly
I am being robbed of my country, an offense to heaven.
        The facts I've told you, Mother, without heaping
great twists of argument. The clever and the humble   495
alike can see that I have spoken right.

CHORUS LEADER

I think, though I am not a Hellene born,
that what you say is argued very well.

ETEOCLES

    If all men saw the fair and wise the same
    men would not have debaters' double strife.   500
    But nothing is like or even among men
    except the name they give—which is not the fact.
          I'll speak to you, Mother, without concealment:
    I'd go to the stars beyond the eastern sky
    or under earth, if I could do one thing,   505
    seize Tyranny, the greatest of the gods.
    I will not choose to give this good thing up
    to any other, rather than keep it myself.
    It's cowardice to let the big thing go
    and settle for the smaller. Besides, I would feel shame   510
    if he should come in arms and sack the land,
    and so achieve his purpose. This would be for Thebes
    disgrace, if fearing spearmen from Mycenae
    I yielded up my scepter for him to hold.
    He should not seek his truce with arms in hand,   515
    for argument can straighten out as much
    as enemy steel can do.
    If he will live here on some other terms,
    he can. But what he asks I will not yield.
    When I can rule should I become his slave?°   520
          So—on with fire, on with swords of war,
    harness the horses, fill the plain with chariots,
    knowing that I will never yield my rule.
    If one must do a wrong, it's best to do it
    pursuing power—otherwise, let's have virtue.   525

CHORUS LEADER

    It isn't right to speak so well of evil.
    That is no good thing, but a bitterness to justice.

JOCASTA

    My son Eteocles, old age is not
    a total misery. Experience helps.
    Sometimes we can speak wiser than the young.   530

Why do you seek after the goddess Ambition?
The worst of all, this goddess, she is unjust.
Often she comes to happy homes and cities,
and when she leaves, she has destroyed their owners,
she after whom you rave. It's better, child,   535
to honor Equality, who ties friends to friends,
cities to cities, allies to allies.
For equality is stable° among men.
If not, the lesser hates the greater force,
and so begins the day of enmity.   540
Equality set up men's weights and measures,
gave them their numbers. And night's sightless eye
equal divides with day the circling year,
while neither, yielding place, resents the other.   545
So sun and night are servants to mankind.
Yet you will not endure to hold your house
in even shares with him? Where's justice then?°

    Why do you honor so much tyrannic power
and think that unjust happiness is great?   550
It's fine to be looked up to? But it's empty.
You want to have much wealth within your halls,
much trouble with it?
And what is "much"? It's nothing but the name.
Sufficiency's enough for men of sense.
Men do not really own their private goods;°   555
we just look after things which are the gods',
and when they will, they take them back again.
Wealth is not steady; it is of a day.

    Come, if I question you a double question,
whether you wish to rule, or to save the city,   560
will you choose to be its tyrant? But if he wins
and the Argive spear beats down the Theban lance,
then you will see this town of Thebes subdued
and many maidens taken off as slaves,
assaulted, ravished, by our enemies.   565

Truly the wealth which now you seek to have°
will mean but grief for Thebes; you're too ambitious.
So much for you.
                    Your turn now, Polynices:
ignorant favors has Adrastus done you,
and you have come in folly to sack your city.   570
Come, if you take this land—heaven forbid it—
by the gods, what trophies can you set to Zeus?
How start the sacrifice for your vanquished country,
and how inscribe your spoils at Inachus' stream?
"Polynices set these shields up to the gods   575
when he had fired Thebes"? Oh, never, son,
be this, or such as this, your fame in Greece!
But if you are worsted and his side wins, then how
shall you go back to Argos, leaving here
thousands of corpses? Some will surely say:
"Adrastus, what a wedding for your daughter!   580
For one girl's marriage we have all been ruined."
You are pursuing evils—one of two—
you will lose the Argives or fail in winning here.
          Both of you, drop excess. When two converge
in single folly, that is worst of all.   585

CHORUS LEADER
    O gods, in some way yet avert these evils
    and make the sons of Oedipus agree!

ETEOCLES
    Mother, it's too late for talking, and this intermission time
    has been wasted; your good purpose can accomplish nothing
        now.
    For we cannot come to terms except as I have laid them
        down: 590
    that I shall hold the scepter of power in this land.
    Leave off your long advisings, now Mother, let me go.
    And as for you—outside these walls, or you shall die.

POLYNICES

What invulnerable someone will lay a sword on me
for slaughter and not find himself receiving death in turn?   595

ETEOCLES

Near enough, he hasn't left you. Do you see these hands of
   mine?

POLYNICES

Oh, I see you. Wealth's a coward and a thing that loves its life.

ETEOCLES

Then why come you with so many for a battle with a no one?

POLYNICES

Oh, a prudent captain's better than a rash one in a war.

ETEOCLES

You can boast, when we've a truce that saves you from your
   death.   600

POLYNICES

So can you. Again I'm claiming rule and the sharing of this
   land.

ETEOCLES

No use to ask. My house shall still be ruled by none but me.

POLYNICES

Holding more than is your portion?

ETEOCLES

                              Yes. Now leave this land at once.

POLYNICES

Altars of our fathers' worship . . .

ETEOCLES

                              —which you come to plunder now!

POLYNICES

. . . hear me!

ETEOCLES

         Which of them will hear you when you
fight your own country?   605

POLYNICES

Temples of the gods who ride white horses . . .

ETEOCLES

        —and who hate you!

POLYNICES

. . . I am driven from my country . . .

ETEOCLES

        —for you came to ruin it!

POLYNICES

. . . wrongfully, O gods.

ETEOCLES

        Don't call on these gods, but Mycenae's!

POLYNICES

Impious by nature . . .

ETEOCLES

        Never have I been my country's foe.

POLYNICES

. . . who drive me off without my portion.

ETEOCLES

        And I'll kill you yet, besides!   610

POLYNICES

Oh, my father, hear my sorrow!

ETEOCLES

        And he hears what you are doing.

POLYNICES

And you, Mother!

ETEOCLES

It's indecent that you speak of her at all.

POLYNICES

O my city!

ETEOCLES

Go to Argos, and call on Lerna's stream.

POLYNICES

I'm going, never worry. Thank you, Mother.

ETEOCLES

Leave the land!

POLYNICES

I am going, but our father, let me see him.

ETEOCLES

You shall not.   615

POLYNICES

Or the girls, our sisters.

ETEOCLES

Never shall you look on them again.

POLYNICES

O my sisters!

ETEOCLES

Now why call them when you are their enemy?

POLYNICES

Fare you very well, my mother.

JOCASTA

Well, I suffer very much.

POLYNICES

I'm no longer a son of yours.

JOCASTA

                  I was born for suffering.

POLYNICES

For this man has done me insult.

ETEOCLES

                 And I stand insulted back.   620

POLYNICES

Where'll you be before the towers?

ETEOCLES

                 And why should you ask that?

POLYNICES

I shall stand against, to kill you.

ETEOCLES

                 I desire the selfsame thing.

JOCASTA

Oh, woe is me, my children, what will you do?

POLYNICES°

                 You'll see.

JOCASTA

Won't you flee your father's cursings?

POLYNICES

                 Let the whole house fall to ruin!
Soon my bloody sword no longer shall be lazy in its sheath.   625
But the land herself who bore me and her gods I call to
    witness,
that dishonored, badly treated, I am thrust outside the land
like a slave, as if I were not a son of Oedipus, as he is.
O my city, if you suffer, lay the blame on him, not me:
I attack against my will, I was thrust away° unwilling.   630
       Apollo of the roadways, and my rooftops, fare you well,

and my friends of youth and statues of the gods we drenched
    with offerings.
I don't know if I shall ever speak a word to you again.
But I still have hope that somehow if the gods are on my side
I shall kill him and be master of this our Theban land.   635

ETEOCLES

Leave this place; your name means "quarrel"
and our father named you well.

(*Exit Jocasta into the palace and Polynices to the side.*)

CHORUS [*singing*]

STROPHE

Tyrian Cadmus came to this land.
Here the heifer bent her legs and fell,   640
proved the oracle, told him here to build
his house on the fertile plain,
where comes the moisture of fair-flowing waters,°   645
Dirce's water over the sprouting furrows, seeded deep,
where his mother bore Bacchus after her marriage with Zeus.   650
He was still a child when the twining ivy came,
green tendrils and all, to cover him over,
to be part of the Bacchic dances of Theban girls   655
and the women who call his name.

ANTISTROPHE

And there the bloody dragon was,
savage monster who guarded Ares' spring,
looked with his roving eyes on its running stream.   660
The beast was slain with a boulder
when Cadmus came seeking water of lustration,
and struck the bloody head with the blows of his monster-slaying
    arm,   665
sowing its teeth in the furrows deep, at unmothered Pallas'
    bidding.°
Then earth sent up armed terror over its surface.   670
Iron-hearted slaughter sent them back again,

and their blood bedewed the land which had briefly showed them
to the shining winds of heaven.   675

On you also I call, Io's child,
Epaphus, son of our mother, and of Zeus,
—with barbarian cry, with barbarian prayers—°   680
come, come to this land!
It was your descendants who founded it,
and the two-named goddesses own it, Kore and dear Demeter,   685
who is ruler of all, nurse of all, the earth.
Epaphus, send us the goddesses of the torch,
defend this land. For the gods all things are easy.

ETEOCLES   *(To an attendant.)*

Go, and bring here Creon, Menoeceus' son,°   690
the brother of Jocasta, my own mother;
tell him I would consult him on private matters
and state affairs before I go to war.
        But he has saved your trouble; here he is.   695
I see him now, he's coming to my house.

                                        (Enter Creon from the side.)

CREON

I've traveled° far, trying to see you, King
Eteocles; round the Cadmean gates
and all their guards I went, to hunt you down.

ETEOCLES

Creon, be sure I wished to see you too.   700
I found the terms of peace from Polynices,
when we discussed them, far from what we need.

CREON

I've heard that he is arrogant toward Thebes,
trusting his new connection and his army.
But this we must leave hanging on the gods.   705
I've come to tell you what's immediate.

ETEOCLES

What's this? I do not know what you will tell.

CREON

We have a prisoner from the Argive side.

ETEOCLES

What does he say that's new from over there?

CREON

He says the Argive host will shortly circle,° 710
armor and all, the old Cadmean town.

ETEOCLES

Then Thebes must bring her arms outside the town.

CREON

But where? Are you too young to see what's needed?

ETEOCLES

Outside the trenches, where they are to fight.

CREON

This land is few in numbers, they are many. 715

ETEOCLES

And well I know that they are bold—in speech.

CREON

Well, Argos has a swelling fame in Greece.

ETEOCLES

Fear not. I'll fill the plain up with their blood.

CREON

I hope so. But I see much labor here.

ETEOCLES

Well, I'll not coop my army within walls. 720

CREON

To take good counsel—this brings victory.

ETEOCLES

You want me to turn to some other roads?

CREON

All of them, lest our fate depend on one.

ETEOCLES

Should we lay ambush and attack at night?

CREON

So, if you failed, you would come safe again. 725

ETEOCLES

Night holds all even, but favors more the daring.

CREON

It's dread to have ill luck under the darkness.

ETEOCLES

A spear attack while they are at their dinner?

CREON

A brief surprise—but we need victory.

ETEOCLES

But Dirce's stream is deep for their retreat. 730

CREON

Nothing's as good as holding on to safety.

ETEOCLES

Suppose we rode against the Argive camp?

CREON

They're well walled in, with chariots around.

ETEOCLES

What shall I do? Give enemies the town?

CREON

No, but take counsel, since you are so clever. 735

ETEOCLES

And what forecounsel's cleverer than mine?

CREON

They say that seven men, as I have heard . . .

ETEOCLES

What's their assignment? This is a small force.

CREON

. . . will lead their companies to assault the gates.

ETEOCLES

What shall we do? Not wait till we are helpless?   740

CREON

You also choose out seven for the gates.

ETEOCLES

To take command of troops, or fight alone?

CREON

With troops, when they have chosen out the best.

ETEOCLES

I see—to ward off scalings of the walls.

CREON

And choose lieutenants; one man can't see all.   745

ETEOCLES

Choosing for courage or for prudent minds?

CREON

Both. Neither's any good without the other.

ETEOCLES

So be it. To the seven-gated walls
I'll go, and set the captains as you say
in equal numbers against their enemies.   750
It would take long, long talk to give each name,
now while the enemy camps outside our walls.
But I will go, my arm shall not be idle.

I hope my brother may be my opponent,°
that I may fight and take him with my spear   755
and kill the man who came to sack my fatherland.

     The marriage of Antigone, my sister,
and your son Haemon, will be your affair
if I should fail. Their earlier betrothal
I ratify, as I move off to war.   760
You are my mother's brother. I need not tell you
to care for her, for my sake and your own.
My father bears the weight of his own folly,
self-blinded. I won't praise this. But his curse
may kill his sons if it is brought to pass.   765

     One thing we haven't done. We should find out
if seer Teiresias has some word for us.
I'll send your son Menoeceus after him,
the boy who has your father's name, to bring him.   770
With kindness he will come to speak to you,
but I have blamed his seercraft and he hates me.
I lay one charge on you, and on the city:°
if our side wins, let never Polynices   775
be buried here in Theban earth. If someone
tries burial, he must die, though he be kin.
So much to you.

     And now to my own followers:
bring out my arms and armor. To the fight
which lies before me now I go with Justice,   780
who will bring victory.° And I pray to Prudence,
most helpful of gods, that she will save this city.

(Exit Eteocles to the side.)

CHORUS [*singing*]

STROPHE

Ares, who brings us trouble, lover of blood and death,
why do you love them, why stand away from Bromius' feasts?   785
Never, when dances are fair and the girls are crowned,
do you loosen your locks and sing to the breath of the pipe

which the Graces have given for dancing. No, you rouse the host,
the armed host of Argos, against our Theban blood.°   790
You dance first in the dance that knows no music.
Not when the thyrsus whirls and the fawn skins are there°
do you come to Ismenus' stream.
But with sound of chariots, clatter of bits and hooves,
you urge the Argives against our earth-sown race,   795
a dancing crowd in arms that swells with shields,
decked in bronze to batter our walls of stone.
Strife is a terrible god, she who has planned
these sufferings for our rulers, the Labdacid kings.°   800

ANTISTROPHE

O glade with the holy foliage, loved by the many beasts,
Artemis' own Cithaeron that wears the snow,
would you had never taken Jocasta's child
and brought to rearing Oedipus, child cast out of his house,
marked by the golden pins. And would that the winged maid,   805
the mountain portent of grief, had never sung her songs,
the Sphinx whose music was no music at all,
who scratched our walls with hoof and claw
and dragged our youth on high
to heaven's height untrodden, she whom Hades sent   810
against the people of Cadmus. And another evil strife,
the strife of Oedipus' children, comes on the town and its homes.
Evil is never good, nor are these lawless sons,   815
their mother's travail, their father's shame.
She came to her kinsman's bed . . .°

EPODE

Earth, you bore, you bore
—I heard the barbarian tale in my home, I heard it well—
the race that grew from the teeth of the crimson-crested monster,   820
Thebes' noblest shame.
And the sons of heaven, they came to Harmonia's marriage;
the walls of Thebes, they rose to Amphion's lyre,
midway between the streams   825

which pour their moisture over the rich green plain
from Dirce and Ismenus.
And Io, my horned mother, was also mother to kings of Thebes.
This city has shifted from one blessing to another, and ever   830
has stood on high, decked with the crowns of Ares.

> *(Enter the prophet Teiresias from the side, led by his*
> *young daughter, accompanied by Menoeceus.)*

TEIRESIAS

Now lead me on, my daughter. You're the eye
for my blind steps, as a star is to a sailor.   835
Now set my path upon the level ground
and lead me lest I stumble. Your father's weak.
Guard my lot-tablets with your maiden hand
which on my holy seat of prophecy   840
I drew when I had marked the oracle birds.
        O young Menoeceus, Creon's son, now tell me,
how far is still our journey to the town,
and to your father? My knees begin to buckle.
I've come so far I hardly can go on.

CREON

Take courage. You have come to harbor now,   845
among your friends. Now hold him up, my son.
Children,° and old men's feet, they need the help
of someone else's hand.

TEIRESIAS

Ah, we are here. Why did you want me, Creon?

CREON

I've not forgotten. But collect your strength,   850
and draw your breath; forget your laboring road.

TEIRESIAS

I am fatigued, since only yesterday
I came here from the town of Erechtheus' sons.
There they had war against Eumolpus' spear,

and I gave Cecrops' children victory.   855
So, as you see, I wear a golden crown,
as first fruit of their plunder from the foe.

CREON

I'll take your crown of victory as an omen.
We're in midwave of danger, as you know,
Danaus' sons against us, strife for Thebes.   860
Our king is gone, dressed in his warrior arms,
against Mycenae's force, Eteocles.
But he enjoined me to find out from you
what we should do in hope to save our city.

TEIRESIAS

As far as he goes, I'd have locked my mouth,   865
withheld the oracles. But at your asking,
I'll tell you. Creon, the land has long been sick,
since Laius made a child against heaven's will,°
and begot poor Oedipus, husband to his mother.
The bloody ruin of his peering eyes   870
is the gods' clever warning unto Greece.
And Oedipus' sons who tried to cloak this up
with the passage of time, as if to escape the gods,
erred in their folly, since they gave their father
neither his rights nor freedom to depart.   875
And so they stung the wretch to savage anger.
Therefore he cursed them terribly indeed,
since he was ailing and, besides, dishonored.
What did I not do, what did I not say?
All the result was hatred from those sons.
Death by their own hands is upon them, Creon;   880
and many corpses fallen over corpses,
        Argive and Cadmean limbs° mingled together
will give the Theban land a bitter mourning.
        You, my poor city, will be buried with them,
if no one is persuaded by my words.   885
This would be best, that none of Oedipus' house°

live in the land as citizen or lord,
since the gods hound them on to spoil the state.
But since the bad is stronger than the good
there is one other way to save the town.   890
But since for me it is not safe to speak
and bitter to those involved for me to state
the cure that yet could save this city, I'll leave.
Farewell. One among many, I will take
whatever comes. What else is there to do?   895

CREON
Stay here, old man.

TEIRESIAS
                              Do not lay hands on me.

CREON
Now wait! Why flee?

TEIRESIAS
                              Luck flees you, not myself.

CREON
Speak the salvation of the town and townsmen.

TEIRESIAS
Now you may wish it; soon you'll wish it not.

CREON
I could not fail to wish my country's safety.   900

TEIRESIAS
You really want to hear, and you are eager?

CREON
What should I be more earnest for than this?

TEIRESIAS
Soon you will hear about my prophecies.
—But first there's something that I need to know.
Where is Menoeceus, he who brought me here?   905

CREON

He isn't far away, he's close to you.

TEIRESIAS

Let him withdraw, far from my prophecies.

CREON

He is my son and will not talk at large.

TEIRESIAS

You wish that I should speak while he is here?

CREON

Yes. He'll be glad to hear of what will save us.   910

TEIRESIAS

Then shall you hear the way of prophecy,
what you must do to save the Theban town.
You must kill Menoeceus for his country's sake,
your child—since you yourself have asked your fate.

CREON

What are you saying? What's your word, old man?   915

TEIRESIAS

Just what it is, and this you needs must do.

CREON

Oh, you have said much evil in short time.

TEIRESIAS

Evil to you, great safety to your city.

CREON

I wasn't listening, didn't hear. City, farewell.

TEIRESIAS

This is no more the man he was. He dodges.   920

CREON

Go, and good-bye. I do not need your seercraft.

TEIRESIAS

Has truth now died because you are unfortunate?

CREON

Oh, by your knees and by your old man's beard . . .

TEIRESIAS

Why fall before me? Accept what can't be changed.

CREON

. . . be quiet; don't reveal this to the town.   925

TEIRESIAS

You tell me to do wrong; I won't keep quiet.

CREON

What will you do? You plan to kill my child?

TEIRESIAS

Others must deal with action. I must speak.

CREON

Why is this curse on me, and on my son?

TEIRESIAS

You are right to ask, and bring me to debate.   930
He must, in that chamber where the earth-born dragon
was born, the watcher over Dirce's streams,
be slaughtered, and so give libation blood
for Cadmus' crime, appeasing Ares' wrath,
who now takes vengeance for his dragon's death.   935
Do this, and Ares will be your ally.
If Earth gets fruit for fruit, and human blood
for her own offspring, then this land shall be
friendly to you, she who sent up the crop
of golden-helmeted Sown Men. One of their race,
child of the dragon's jaws, must die this death.   940
You are the one survivor of the Sown,
pure-blooded, on both sides, you and your sons.
Haemon's betrothal saves him from the slaughter.°

For he is not unwedded, though still virgin. 945
This boy, who belongs to none but to the city,
if he would die, will save his fatherland,
make harsh homecoming for Adrastus and the Argives,
casting the dark of night upon their eyes, 950
and make Thebes famous. There you have your choice,
to save your city or to save your son.

     Now you have all I know. Child, take me home.
A man's a fool to use the prophet's trade.
For if he happens to bring bitter news 955
he's hated by the men for whom he works;
and if he pities them and tells them lies
he wrongs the gods. No prophet but Apollo
should sing to men, for he has none to fear.

                    (*Exit Teiresias and his daughter to the side.*)

CHORUS LEADER

Creon, why are you silent, holding your tongue? 960
Myself, I'm no less stricken and amazed.

CREON

What can one say? But my response is clear.
I'll never walk into such wretchedness
as to give my city the slaughter of my son.
It's part of human life to love one's children. 965
No one would give his own son up to death.
Let no one praise me who would kill my sons!
Though I, since I am in the prime of life,
am ready to die to set my country free.

     Up, son, before the whole town learns of this, 970
pay no attention to these wanton bodings,
fly quickly, get yourself outside this land.
For he will tell this to the chiefs and captains,°
making the rounds of the gates and their commanders.
If we anticipate him, you are safe. 975
If you come second, we're destroyed, you die.

MENOECEUS

Where shall I flee, to what city and what friend?

CREON

As far away from here as you can get.

MENOECEUS

You'd better tell me where, and I will do it.

CREON

Go beyond Delphi . . .

MENOECEUS

                                And where on beyond?   980

CREON

. . . into Aetolia.

MENOECEUS

                        And where after that?

CREON

Thesprotia's plain.

MENOECEUS

                        Where holy Dodona stands?

CREON

Yes.

MENOECEUS

        What protection will that be for me?

CREON

The god will guide you.

MENOECEUS

                        And for my supplies?

CREON

I'll give you gold.

You talk good sense, my father.   985

Go get it then. I'll go to see your sister
Jocasta, she who nursed me at her breast,
when my mother died and I was left an orphan.
I'll visit her, then go and save my life.
Please hurry now, may you not be delayed.°   990

(Exit Creon to the side.)

Women, how well I've taken away his fear,
cheating with words, to get what I desire.
He'd steal me out, robbing the state of safety,
give me to cowardice. This could be forgiven
in an old man, but not pardoned in myself,   995
that I should so betray my fatherland.
Know well, I'm going, and I'll save the town
and give my life to death to save this land.
How shameful if men who are not under omens,
and so constrained by heaven's necessity,   1000
stand at their shields and do not shrink at death,
fighting before the towers for their country—
while I, betraying my father and my brother
and my own city, leave the land, a coward.
Wherever I'd live, I'd show myself a weakling.   1005
By Zeus, among the stars, and bloody Ares,
who set the Sown Men, offspring of this land,
to be its rulers, I am going now.
I'll take my stand on the high battlements
over that precinct where the dragon lived,
there slay myself above its gloomy depths   1010
that the seer spoke of; so I'll free the land.
I've said my say, and now I go to give°
my city no mean gift. I'll cure this ailing land.
If every man would take what good he can   1015
and contribute it to his city's common good,
cities would suffer less, be happy from now on.

(Exit Menoeceus to the side.)

CHORUS [*singing*]

STROPHE

You came, you came,
you wingèd thing, Earth's offspring, monster's child,   1020
to seize the sons of Cadmus:
half a maiden, a fearful beast,
with roving wings and claws that fed on blood.   1025
You who snatched the youths from Dirce's plain,
crying your Fury's shriek,
the song that knows no music,
you brought, you brought sorrows upon our land,   1030
bloody ones—and bloody was the god
who brought these things about.
Mournings of the mothers,
mournings of the maidens,
filled our homes with grief.   1035
Groan and cry ran back and forth
from one to another through the town,
like thunder they groaned   1040
each time the wingèd maiden seized one of the city's men.

ANTISTROPHE

In time there came
—the Pythian sent him—Oedipus the wretched,
here to this land of Thebes.   1045
First we were glad, but later we grieved.
He conquered the riddle; poor wretch, he wed his mother.
He stained the town and through slaughter he came to strife,   1050
casting the curse on his sons.
We praise him who goes,
we praise the man who is dying to save his land.   1055
Lament he leaves to Creon.
But to the town's seven gates
he brings a glorious triumph.
Pallas, make us mothers   1060

of sons as good as this,
you who checked the dragon blood,
by the rock you urged Cadmus to throw.
Yet from this victory came   1065
a curse of god on this land, and slaughter with it.

(Enter one of Eteocles' soldiers as Messenger from the side.)

MESSENGER   (Calling at the door of the palace.)
You there, whoever's watching at the gate,
open, and bring Jocasta from the house.
Open, I say! You've waited long, but now
come forth and listen, famed wife of Oedipus,°   1070
leaving your wailing and your tears of grief.

(Enter Jocasta from the palace.)

JOCASTA
Dear friend, you haven't come to tell disaster,
Eteocles' death, you who march by his shield,
constantly keeping off the enemy shafts?
What is the new word that you bring to me?°   1075
Is my son alive or dead? Now tell me true.

MESSENGER
He lives, so tremble not, that fear is gone.

JOCASTA
How is the circuit of the seven gates?

MESSENGER
They stand unbroken, the city is not plundered.

JOCASTA
Were they endangered by the Argive spear?   1080

MESSENGER
Right on the verge. But our Cadmean Ares
was stronger than the Mycenaean spear.

JOCASTA

By the gods, tell one thing more! What do you know
of Polynices? I care for his life too.

MESSENGER

Both of your sons are living to this moment.   1085

JOCASTA

God bless you! How, when you were sore besieged,
did you force back the Argives from the gates?
Tell me, that I may please the blind old man,
sitting inside, with news of the city's rescue.

MESSENGER

When Creon's son, who died to save the city,   1090
on the highest tower standing, had thrust his sword
through his own throat and saved this land of ours,
your son sent seven companies and their captains,
to the seven gates, to keep the Argives off.
Horses against the horsemen did he set,   1095
foot against infantry, so where the wall
was weak against assault, he guarded it.
From the high citadel we saw the host,
white-shielded men of Argos. They left Teumessus,   1100
they rushed the ditch to set the town on fire.°
Then the paean and the trumpet played together,
from there, and from our walls.
Then first attacked were the Neïstan gates°
by a company bristling with its thick-set shields.   1105
Parthenopaeus led them, the huntress' child.
A fitting sign was blazing on his shield,
Atalanta with her distant-ranging arrows
killing Aetolia's boar. Against the gate
of Proetus came the seer, Amphiaraus,
with sacrificial offerings on his car,   1110
modestly, no insolent sign on his blank shield.
Against the Ogygian gate the lord Hippomedon

came with a sign in the middle of his shield,
the All-Seeing one, with eyes all over him, 1115
some eyes that look forth as the stars come up,
others that hide among the setting stars,
as later we could see when the man was dead.
Against Homoloid gate Tydeus took his stand.
He bore a lion's hide upon his shield 1120
with bristling mane, and like Prometheus held
in his right hand a torch to burn the town.
Your Polynices by the Gate of Springs
led on the war. Upon his shield the fillies
of Potniae raged and ran in panic fear, 1125
moving by pivots near the handle grip.
They did seem mad indeed.
And he who loves war even as Ares does,
Capaneus led against the Electran gate.
The iron markings on his shield were these: 1130
an earth-born Giant carried on his shoulders
a whole town wrenched away from its foundations,
this to suggest what our town would endure.
Adrastus himself was at the seventh gate.
A hundred snakes were pictured on his shield. 1135
Yes, on his left arm rode the Argive Hydras.
And from our walls these snakes, with snatching jaws,
were taking Cadmus' children.
Now all these things I very well could see
since it was I who took the password round. 1140
        So first we fought with arrows and throwing-spears
and far-flung slingshots and the crash of stones.
When we had won this fighting, Tydeus cried,
sudden, so did your son, "O Danaan men,
do not delay, before their shafts have shredded you, 1145
charge at the gates, light-armed, and horse, and chariots."
And when they heard the cry, no man was slow,
and many fell, their heads bedaubed with blood,
while from our walls you could have seen large numbers 1150

dive to the plain and breathe their life away.
They dewed the thirsty earth with streams of blood.

      Then that Arcadian, Atalanta's son,
no Argive, rushed upon the gates a storm,
crying for double axes and for fire,
meaning to overturn our town. But then   1155
the sea god's son, Periclymenus, cast a stone,
a wagon's load, from the high cornice-top,
broke up his yellow head, shattered the joinings
of bone on bone; straightway his blushing face   1160
blushed with his blood. He'll not return alive
to the queen of archers, his mother, the mountain maid.

      When he had seen that this gate was defended,
your son went on, I followed, and I saw
Tydeus and many shieldmen by his side   1165
dashing Aetolian spears against the top
of our defenses, so that many fled
the upper battlements. But against him too
your son brought on the crowd as a huntsman does
and saved the towers. So to the next gate   1170
we hurried on, having stopped the sickness there.

      How can I tell you how Capaneus raged?
For he came with the steps of a long ladder.
This was his boast, that Zeus's awful fire   1175
could not hold him back from overturning the city.
He cried this as they threw the stones against him,
and still climbed up the ladder, coiled within
his shield, step after step, and rung by rung.
Just as he reached the cornice of the wall   1180
Zeus struck with lightning, and the earth rang out
so all were frightened. From the ladder he fell,
limbs whirling like a sling. His hair streamed high;°
his blood fell down to earth. His arms and legs
went spinning like Ixion on his wheel.   1185
He fell upon the ground a flaming corpse.

      When Adrastus saw Zeus was his enemy,

he drew his army back behind the ditch.
But we, who saw the omen on our side,
horsemen and chariots and infantry rushed out.   1190
We drove our spears into their very center.
Ruin was everywhere. They died, they fell
down from the chariot's rim. The wheels rebounded.
Axle on axle, corpse on corpse was heaped.   1195
         This land's defenses have been kept from ruin
this day. The gods must see if this our land
remains successful. For some god has saved her.°

CHORUS LEADER
    How fair is victory! If the gods have still°   1200
    a better plan, I'll hope for my own fortune.

JOCASTA
    The gods and fortune both have served us well.
    My sons are alive. The country has escaped.
    But Creon, he has reaped a mournful harvest,   1205
    who married me to Oedipus. Gone is his son:
    good fortune for the town, a grief to him.
    Go on now, tell me what my sons will do.

MESSENGER
    Let be the rest. So far your fortune holds.

JOCASTA
    Suspicious sayings. This I'll not allow.   1210

MESSENGER
    What more do you want than to know your sons are saved?

JOCASTA
    To hear if I have happiness in the future.

MESSENGER
    Let me go. I'm your son's attendant, and he needs me.

JOCASTA
    You hide some evil and cover it up in dark.

MESSENGER

I would not add your sorrows to your gains.   1215

JOCASTA

You must, unless you fly away to heaven.

MESSENGER

Alas, why not let me leave good news behind me?
Why force me to tell the bad?
Your sons intend—oh shamefulness of daring!—
a single combat, severed from the host.   1220
And they have said to Argives and Cadmeans°
words which they never should have said at all.
Eteocles began. High on a tower,
he ordered that the army be called to silence
and said, "O leaders of the land of Hellas,   1225
lords of the Danaans, you who here have come,
and Cadmus' people, not for Polynices
nor for myself should you exchange your lives.
For I myself, putting this danger off,
alone will join in battle with my brother.   1230
If I kill him, I'll hold my house alone;
if I am worsted, to him alone I'll yield it.
Give up the struggle, Argives: you'll depart
this land without leaving your own lives here;
and of the Sown Men there are already dead enough."   1235
         So much he said, and your son Polynices
straightway leapt up and praised what he had said.
And all the Argives shouted their approval,
and Cadmus' people, for they thought it just.
So truce was made. In no-man's-land the chiefs   1240
took solemn oath they would abide by it.
         Then did they cover their bodies with brazen arms,
the two young sons of the old Oedipus.
Their friends were arming them. The Theban lords
saw to our captain, the Argive chiefs to the other.   1245
Then they stood shining, and they had not paled

but raged to cast their spears at one another.
And from about their friends came up to them,
cheered them with speech and said such words as these:
"Polynices, now you can set up for Zeus   1250
his triumph statue and make Argos famed."
To Eteocles: "Now you are fighting for your city;
now when you conquer, you will hold the rule."
        Such things they said, exhorting them to battle.
The seers slew sheep and marked the points of flame,   1255
its cleavages, any damp signs of evil,
and that high shining which may have two meanings,
a mark of victory, or of the losing side.
If you have strength or any words of wisdom
or spells of incantation, go, hold back   1260
your children from dread strife. The danger's great.
Your dreadful prize will only be your tears°
if you should lose both sons this very day.

JOCASTA [*calling into the palace*]
My child Antigone, come outside the house.
No help for you in maidens' works and dances.°   1265
The gods have set it so. But those brave men
your brothers, who are rushing on their death,
you and your mother must keep from mutual murder.

                    (*Enter Antigone from the palace.*)

ANTIGONE
Mother, what new terror for our family   1270
do you cry out before the palace front?

JOCASTA
Daughter, your brothers' lives are falling fast.

ANTIGONE
What do you say?

JOCASTA
                    They're set for single fight.

ANTIGONE
Oh no! What words are these?

JOCASTA
                    Hard words. Follow me.

ANTIGONE
Where, as I leave my chamber?

JOCASTA
                    To the armies.   1275

ANTIGONE
I fear the crowd.

JOCASTA
                    Modesty will not help.

ANTIGONE
What shall I do?

JOCASTA
                    Undo your brothers' strife.

ANTIGONE
But how?

JOCASTA
                    By supplicating them, with me.

                              (To the Messenger.)

Lead us to the battlefield. We can't delay.°
You hurry, hurry, daughter. If I catch them   1280
before they raise their spears, my life's in light.°
But if they die, I'll lie with them in death.

              (Exit Jocasta, Antigone, and the Messenger to the side.)

CHORUS [*singing*]
                    STROPHE
Alas, alas, my shuddering heart!

Pity, pity goes through my flesh　　　　　　　　1285
as I think of that wretched mother.
Which of her children will kill her child
—Oh, the sufferings, Zeus, Oh Earth—　　　　　1290
cutting his brother's throat, spilling his brother's breath?
And I, poor soul, which corpse shall I lament?　　1295

ANTISTROPHE

Woe, oh woe, twin beasts!
Bloody spirits, shaking the spear,
how soon they will work their murders!
Unhappy that ever they thought of this duel.　　　1300
With barbarian wailings I'll mourn the dead.
The fortune of death is near, the sword° will show what comes.
This murder the Furies have wrought is a fate beyond all fates.　1305

CHORUS LEADER

But I see Creon coming to the house
with clouded face, and break off this lament.

(*Enter from the side Creon, and attendants
carrying the body of Menoeceus.*)

CREON°

What shall I do? And should my tears lament　　　1310
myself, or this poor city, held in gloom
as if it traveled down to Acheron?
My child has perished, dying for this land.
The name he leaves is noble, but sad for me.
Just now I took him from the dragon rocks,　　　1315
took in my arms my son who killed himself.
My whole house mourns. And I, in my old age,
I come for my old sister, Queen Jocasta,
to lay my son out for his funeral.
For to the dead we who are not yet dead　　　　1320
must pay respect, honoring the god below.

CHORUS LEADER

Gone is your sister, Creon, from the house,
and with her went the maid Antigone.

CREON

Where? And what trouble called them? Tell me now.

CHORUS LEADER

She heard her sons were planning single fight   1325
with spear and shield over the royal house.

CREON

What are you saying? This I had not heard,
since I was caring for my own son's corpse.

CHORUS LEADER

Your sister left the house some time ago.
I think the mortal combat of those sons,   1330
Oedipus' sons, is at an end by now.

(Enter a Messenger from the side.)

CREON

Alas, indeed I see a sign of that:
the dark and scowling face of one who comes
to bring the news of everything that's happened.

MESSENGER

Woe is me, how tell my story or the groaning that I bring?   1335

CREON

We are ruined, I can tell it from the gloom with which you
     start.

MESSENGER

"Woe is me," I cry again, for the trouble I bring is great.

CREON

To be heaped upon the sufferings we had suffered. What's
     your news?

MESSENGER

Creon, your sister's children are no longer in the light.

CREON [singing]

Alas!   1340
Great is the sorrow you bring, for me and for the city.
O house of Oedipus, have you heard the news?
Your sons have perished, both in one disaster.

CHORUS LEADER

The house would weep, if it could understand.

CREON [singing]

Alas, disaster, born of heavy fate!   1345
Ah, for my sorrows, how I suffer now!

MESSENGER

And if you knew the further misery!

CREON [now speaking]

How could there be a worser fate than this?

MESSENGER

Your sister died along with her two sons.

CHORUS [singing]

Lead off the wailing, batter your head in mourning   1350
with your fair white arms!

CREON

Jocasta, what an ending to your life,
and to your marriage, caused by the Sphinx's riddle.

CHORUS LEADER°

Tell me about the slaughter of the sons,
the working-out in fight of Oedipus' curse.   1355

MESSENGER

You know our first good fortune before the towers,
for the city walls are not so far away
you couldn't see the things that happened there.

When they were fitted with their shining arms,
the two young sons of Oedipus the old,   1360
they rose and went into the middle plain,
the two commanders, the pair of generals,°
for the struggle of the single fight in arms.
Looking toward Argos Polynices prayed,
"O lady Hera, yours I am: I'm wed   1365
to Adrastus' child and living in your land.
Grant I may kill my brother, so my hand
show sign of victory, my opponent's blood."
He asked a shameful crown, his brother's death.°
Tears came to many at this monstrous prayer,   1370
men looked at one another in the crowd.
Eteocles prayed, looking toward the house
of golden-shielded Pallas, "Daughter of Zeus,
grant me to drive my spear in victory
into my brother's breast with this my arm,   1375
to kill the one who came to sack my land."°
        Then the Tyrrhenian trumpet-blast burst forth,
like fire, as the signal for the fight;
they ran a dreadful race at one another
and like wild boars that sharpen their savage tusks   1380
drew close, both foaming slaver down their beards.
Both lunged with spears, but drew within their shields
so that the steel might spend itself in vain.
If either saw the other's eye peer up
above the rim, he darted with his spear,
hoping to catch him quickly with its point.   1385
But both were clever, peering through the shield slits,
so neither's spear was any use at all.
We who were watching sweated more than they,°
all fearful for our friends.
        Eteocles slipped a little on a stone
that turned beneath his foot. One leg came out   1390
around the shield; and Polynices struck,
seeing the mark thus offered to his steel.

The Argive spear went cleanly through his calf
and all the Danaan army cried in joy.   1395
And Eteocles, wounded,° saw his brother's shoulder
exposed in the struggle, and he struck at that.
Thebans rejoiced; but the spearhead broke off short.
His spear no use, he fell back step by step,   1400
then seized and hurled a rugged rock which broke
his brother's spear, so now on even terms
they stood, since neither had a lance in hand.
      Then snatching at the handles of their swords
they came together, and they clashed their shields,   1405
pushed back and forth, and frightful was the noise.
Eteocles, who'd been to Thessaly,
had learned and used a fine Thessalian trick.
He disentangled from their present struggle,
fell with his left foot back, watching his mark   1410
in his foe's belly. Then he jumped ahead
on his right foot and struck him in the navel.
The sword went through and reached right to the spine.
Stooped over his belly Polynices fell   1415
with gasps of blood. The victor stuck his sword
into the earth, began to strip his arms,
not mindful of himself, only of that.
This was his finish. The other had some life left,
had kept his sword all through his painful fall.   1420
Scarcely he managed, but he thrust that sword,
he the first-fallen, through his brother's liver.
They bit the dust and lie near one another;
the two divided thus their heritage.

CHORUS LEADER
  O Oedipus, how much I mourn your woes.   1425
  It seems a god has now fulfilled your curse.

MESSENGER
  Hear now the woes that followed upon these.
  Just as her fallen children left this life

their wretched mother came upon them both,°
she in her hurry, with her daughter too.   1430
And when she saw them with their mortal wounds,
she groaned, "O children, I bring help too late."
Falling upon her children, each in turn,
she wept, she mourned them, all her nursing wasted.
Their sister at her side like a warrior's helper   1435
cried, "O supporters of our mother's age,
you have betrayed my marriage, dearest brothers."
Eteocles' hard dying breath was coming
out from his chest, and yet he heard his mother,
laid his damp hand on hers. He could not speak.
But tears fell from his eyes in sign of love.   1440
The other had breath, and looking toward his sister
and his old mother, Polynices said:
"Mother, we're dead. I pity you indeed,
and this my sister and my brother's corpse,   1445
my friend turned enemy, but still my friend.
Mother, and you, my sister, bury me
in my own land. Persuade the angry city
to grant me this much of my father's soil,
though I got not our house. Close up my eyes,   1450
Mother," he said, and put her hand upon them.
"Farewell, the darkness now is closing in."
        So both together breathed out their sad lives.
But their mother, when she looked on this disaster   1455
snatched a sword off the corpses and she did
a dreadful deed. Straight through her neck she drove
the steel. So now she lies among her own.
In death her arms are cast about them both.
        Then did the armies rush to strife of words,   1460
we claiming that my master won the day,
and they the other. The captains quarreled too.
Some claimed that Polynices' spear struck first,°
the others that dead men have no victory.
Meanwhile, Antigone had left the army.   1465

They rushed for weapons, but by prudent forethought
the Theban host had halted under arms.
So we fell on them not yet in their armor,
swooping upon the Argive host in haste.
No one withstood us, they fled, and filled the plain.   1470
Blood flowed from myriad corpses slain by spears.
When we had conquered, some set up for Zeus
his trophy statue, others stripped the corpses
and sent the shields within the walls as spoils.   1475
And others, with Antigone, bring the dead
so their own friends may give them mourning here.
Of these sad contests, some have ended well
for this our city, others ill indeed.

(Exit Messenger to the side. Enter Antigone from the other side, with
attendants bearing the bodies of the two brothers and of Jocasta.)

CHORUS [chanting]
No longer for hearing alone   1480
is the city's grief. You may see
the three dead on their way
near to the palace, they who found
together their darkened end.

ANTIGONE [singing]
No veil now covers the curls on my delicate cheek,   1485
nor in maiden shame have I hidden the blush on my face.
I come as a Bacchant, celebrating death.
I have thrown the veil from my hair, my saffron robe hangs loose.   1490
I bring on the dead with my groans.
O Polynices, you followed your quarreling name.
Woe it was for Thebes; and your strife, which was more than strife   1495
but ended as murder on murder, has brought the end
of Oedipus' house in dreadful blood,
in terrible blood.
What singer, what singers, O house,   1500
shall I call for this song of grief,

I who bring three kindred bloodily dead,
mother and children, the Fury's delight?
Delight of her who has ruined the house entire,
Oedipus' house; and the ruin began   1505
when he unriddled the riddling song
of the singing Sphinx and slew her dead.
O Father, woe for you!
What Greek or foreigner,
what man of a noble race   1510
has suffered so many bloody griefs so clear to see?
My poor self, how my song rings out!°
What bird that sits
in the oak or the high twigs of the fir tree   1515
will join my lamenting,
alone, without my mother,
helping the song of my grief.
Woe for the wailings with which I mourn,
I who shall live my life alone   1520
among my falling tears.
On which of them first
shall I cast the first fruits
of my shorn-off hair?   1525
On my mother's two breasts
where I drew my milk,
or the horrible wounds of my brothers?
Oh, oh, come forth from the house,   1530
with your blinded face,
old father Oedipus, show your wretched self,
you who drag out a wretched long life
after casting the dark on your eyes.°   1535
Do you hear me,
wandering old-footed in the courtyard,
or are you lying wretched in bed?

(Enter Oedipus from the palace.)

OEDIPUS [*singing throughout this lyric interchange with Antigone, who
sings in response*]
　　Why have you brought me forth to the light,　　　　　　　1540
　　dragging my blindness along on a stick,
　　with your pitiful tears, from my bed in the dark,
　　a gray, invisible ghost of the air, a corpse, a flying dream?　　　1545

ANTIGONE
　　You must hear the telling of dreadful news.
　　Father, your sons are dead.
　　And so is the wife who tended and guided your stumbling steps,
　　O Father, woe is me.　　　　　　　　　　　　　　1550

OEDIPUS
　　Woe for my frightful griefs. I must moan, I must cry aloud.
　　Three lives gone! My child,
　　how did they leave the light; what was the fate that fell?

ANTIGONE
　　Not in reproach do I say it, nor glad at your grief,　　　　　1555
　　but in simple sorrow: the avenging power of your curse,
　　heavy with swords and fire and wicked fightings, fell,
　　Father, on your sons.

OEDIPUS
　　Alas!

ANTIGONE
　　　　Why this lament?　　　　　　　　　　　　　1560

OEDIPUS
　　My children!

ANTIGONE
　　　　You are in grief.
　　But, Father, if you could see the chariot of the sun
　　and cast your eyes on these corpses!

OEDIPUS

It's clear what disaster came on my sons. 1565
But what doom struck down my wife?

ANTIGONE

She showed all men her groaning tears.
She went to her sons as a suppliant, to adjure them by her breast.
Their mother found them like lions wild,
wielding their spears in war with each other.
There in the flowering meadow,° 1570
beside Electra's gate,
they were fighting and wounded; already the blood
was running to make them cold, 1575
Hades' libation, which Ares grants.
So taking the bronze-hammered sword from the dead,
she plunged it into her flesh, and in grief for her sons,
she fell on their corpses.
The god who brought this about
has brought together all of these griefs for our house, 1580
Father, in one short day.

CHORUS LEADER°

This day has started very many sorrows
for Oedipus' house. May our own life be better!

CREON

Cease from your mourning. Now it is the time
to think of burial. Oedipus, hear this speech: 1585
Eteocles, your son, gave me the rule
over this land, and made that rule the dowry
for Haemon's marriage with Antigone.
I will not let you live here any more,
for clearly has Teiresias said that never, 1590
while you are here, can the city prosper well.
So, on your way! This proclamation comes
not as an insult, nor am I your enemy.

I simply fear that the Avengers who pursue you
may do more damage to this land of ours.

OEDIPUS [*now speaking*]

O fate, you bred me wretched from the start   1595
for suffering, if ever mortal was.
Before I came to light from my mother's womb
Apollo prophesied that I, the unborn,
should kill my father—suffering indeed.
Once I was born, the father who begot me,
counting me as his enemy, tried to kill me,   1600
since he must die through me, and so he sent me,
still a breast-loving baby, to be food
for the wild beasts.
There was I saved. Cithaeron, you should sink
in the depthless chasms of the underworld,   1605
you who did not destroy me, but a god
gave me in servitude to Polybus.
So when, ill-fated, I had killed my father,
I came into my wretched mother's bed
and begot brother-sons whom now I've killed,   1610
passing on to my children Laius' curse.
For I am not so foolish in my nature
as to do what I did to my eyes, and to their lives,
if it were not some god who had contrived it.
        Well, what's to do now with my wretched self?   1615
Who is to guide this blind man? She who's dead?
Full well I know, were she alive, she would.
Or my good pair of sons? They are no more.
Am I still young enough to make my living?
From what? Creon, why kill me utterly?
For you are killing me if you cast me out.   1620
Yet I'll not clutch your knees and prove a coward.
Even in misery, I won't betray my birth.

CREON

It is well spoken not to grasp my knees;   1625

I shall not let you live within this land.

      Now, of these dead, the one must straight be taken
into the house. The other, he who came
to sack his fatherland with foreign help,
that Polynices, do you cast his corpse
beyond the boundaries of this land unburied.   1630
And this shall be proclaimed to all the Thebans:
"Whoever lays a wreath upon this corpse
or buries him, shall find reward in death.
Leave him unwept, unburied, food for the birds."

      And you, Antigone, leave your triple dirge   1635
and come inside the house. For the time being
you'll stay a maiden, but before long Haemon
and marriage are for you.

ANTIGONE [*now speaking*]
Father, what wretchedness is on us now!
I mourn for you still more than for the dead.   1640
For yours is not mixed grief heavy and light;
but you are perfect in your misery.

      But you, new ruler, I would ask you this:
Why wrong my father, sending him from the land?
Why lay down laws against a pitiful corpse?   1645

CREON
This was Eteocles' decision, and not mine.

ANTIGONE
Senseless. And you a fool to follow it.

CREON
Is it not right to do what is commanded?

ANTIGONE
Not when the orders are wrong and wickedly spoken.

CREON
Is it not right to give him to the dogs?   1650

ANTIGONE

The punishment you seek is not the law's.

CREON

It is, for the city's foe who was our friend.

ANTIGONE

But didn't he yield his life up to his fate?

CREON

And therefore let him yield his burial.

ANTIGONE

What was his crime to seek his share of earth?   1655

CREON

Be sure, this man is going to lie unburied.

ANTIGONE

Then I shall bury him, though the state forbids.

CREON

Then will you bury yourself close by that corpse.

ANTIGONE

It's glorious that two kin should lie together.

CREON

Lay hold of her and take her to the house.   1660

ANTIGONE

Oh no! I will not loose my hold on him.

CREON

The gods' these judgments, and not yours, my girl.

ANTIGONE

And it is not judged right to outrage a corpse.

CREON

No one shall lay the damp dust over him.

ANTIGONE

They will. I swear it for Jocasta's sake. 1665

CREON

You toil in vain. You cannot get your wish.

ANTIGONE

At least allow me but to bathe his body.

CREON

This too shall be forbidden by the state.

ANTIGONE

But then to bandage up his savage wounds.

CREON

There is no honor you may give this corpse. 1670

ANTIGONE

O dearest, but at least I kiss your mouth.

CREON

Don't mar your marriage with these lamentations.

ANTIGONE

Do you think that I shall live to wed your son?

CREON

You'll be forced to it. What refuge from his bed?

ANTIGONE

That night will make me one with the Danaids. 1675

CREON

Do you see the daring of her insolence?

ANTIGONE

Let the steel know. My oath is by the sword.

CREON

Why do you wish so to avoid this marriage?

ANTIGONE

I'll go to exile with my wretched father.

CREON

You show nobility, as well as folly.   1680

ANTIGONE

And know you well that I will die with him.

CREON

Go! You'll not kill my son. Now leave the land.

(*Exit Creon into the palace.*)

OEDIPUS

Daughter, I praise your loving zeal for me.

ANTIGONE

How could I marry and send you alone to exile?

OEDIPUS

Stay and be happy. I will bear my woes.   1685

ANTIGONE

But you are blind. Who'll care for you, my father?

OEDIPUS

Where fate decides it I will fall and lie.

ANTIGONE

Ah, where is Oedipus and his famous riddle?

OEDIPUS

Perished. One day blessed me, and one day ruined.

ANTIGONE

Should I not have some part in all your troubles?   1690

OEDIPUS

Exile with a blind father is disgrace.

ANTIGONE

Not for the dutiful. Then it is an honor.

OEDIPUS

Now lead me forward, that I may touch your mother.

ANTIGONE

There. Lay your hand upon that dear old woman.

OEDIPUS

O Mother, O unhappy wife of mine!   1695

ANTIGONE

She lies there piteous, having suffered all.

OEDIPUS

Where is Eteocles' corpse, and Polynices'?

ANTIGONE

Here lie they, stretched out close to one another.

OEDIPUS

Put my unseeing hand upon their faces.

ANTIGONE

There. Lay your hand upon your sons in death.   1700

OEDIPUS

O dear dead sons, unhappy as your father!

ANTIGONE

O Polynices, dearest name to me.

OEDIPUS

Now Loxias' doom is working to its end.

ANTIGONE

What is it? Further woes on top of woes?

OEDIPUS

That, wandering, I shall die on Attic soil.   1705

ANTIGONE

Where? Which of Athens' forts will shelter you?

OEDIPUS

Sacred Colonus, where the horse god lives.

But come, help your blind father on his way,
since you are eager to be exiled with me.

ANTIGONE [*singing henceforth with Oedipus, who sings in reply*]
On to our exile. Father, stretch out your hand.　　　　　　1710
I help your steps as the wind helps on the ship.

OEDIPUS
I come, I come.
Oh my poor child, now lead me.

ANTIGONE
I do, I do, most wretched I,
of all the girls of Thebes.

OEDIPUS
Where shall I set my old foot?　　　　　　　　　　　　1715
Daughter, give me my staff.

ANTIGONE
This way, this way, with me.
Like this, like this, your feet.　　　　　　　　　　　　1720
Your strength is like a dream.

OEDIPUS
Oh me, oh me, who am driven, an ancient man,
in exile from my land.
What terrible things I have suffered!　　　　　　　　　1725

ANTIGONE
Why of your suffering speak? Justice regards not the wicked.
She gives no prizes for folly.

OEDIPUS
And I am the one who reached the heights of song.
When I found out the maiden's riddle, no fool was I.　　　1730

ANTIGONE
You go back to the Sphinx, and our shame.
Stop speaking of past good fortune.

There awaits you pitiful suffering   1735
and, somewhere, an exile's death.

And I leave tears for the girls my friends
as I part from my fatherland
to wander, unmaidenly.

OEDIPUS
Alas for your honest heart!   1740

ANTIGONE
It will give me fame concerning my father's sorrows.
I mourn for your wrongs, and for those which are done my brother,
who goes from the house a corpse to lie unburied.
Father, even if I must die,
in secret I'll bury that body.   1745

OEDIPUS
Return again to your friends!

ANTIGONE
My own laments are enough.

OEDIPUS
You can pray to the holy altars.

ANTIGONE
They have had enough of my troubles.   1750

OEDIPUS
Then go to Bacchus' shrine in the hills
where none but the maenads are!

ANTIGONE
To go where once I went
in Theban fawnskin clad,   1755
and danced in Semele's holy choir!
It was a graceless grace I did the gods.

OEDIPUS [now speaking]
You that live in my ancestral Thebes, behold this Oedipus,°

him who knew the famous riddles and who was a man most
     great.
It was I alone put down the murdering power of the Sphinx.   1760
Now it's I who go dishonored in sad exile from the land.
Yet why do I lament these things and mourn for them in
     vain?
The constraint the gods lay on us we mortals all must bear.

(Exit Oedipus and Antigone to the side.)

CHORUS [*chanting*]
   O great Victory, stay with me°
   all my life.   1765
   Nor cease to give me crowns!

ORESTES

Translated by WILLIAM ARROWSMITH

ORESTES: INTRODUCTION

The Play: Date and Composition

Euripides' *Orestes* was first produced in 408 BCE for the annual competition at the Great Dionysian Festival in Athens. What the other three plays were in Euripides' tetralogy of that year, and how they fared in the dramatic competition, are unknown.

The Myth

Orestes presents an episode from the tragic vicissitudes of the house of the Pelopids, involving the royal dynasties of Argos (or Mycenae) and Sparta: Atreus' son Agamemnon, Agamemnon's wife Clytemnestra, her lover Aegisthus, and her children Iphigenia, Electra, and Orestes, along with Agamemnon's brother Menelaus, his Spartan wife Helen (Clytemnestra's sister), and their daughter Hermione. The story is best known to ancient and modern audiences alike from Aeschylus' *Oresteia*. After Agamemnon returned from sacking Troy and helping his brother recover Helen, Clytemnestra and Aegisthus murdered him; and then Orestes, at the behest of Apollo, killed Clytemnestra and Aegisthus in turn.

It is at this point that the action of Euripides' play begins. When Orestes, who is suffering from bouts of madness for his crime, and Electra are condemned to death by the Argive assembly for matricide, they decide, prompted by Orestes' comrade Pylades, to murder Helen in order to make their enemies suffer too, and then to seize Hermione as a hostage and to threaten to set fire to the palace so as to coerce Menelaus into persuading the Argives to let them live. Orestes and Pylades enter the palace to put this plan into effect. After much confusion, Apollo appears above the palace to explain that Helen has been rescued and deified, and to predict the future: Orestes will be tried and acquitted in Athens, and he will marry Hermione, be reconciled with Menelaus, and rule Argos. All ends, seemingly, well.

Other episodes in the history of the House of Atreus were brought onto the stage by many other tragedians, including Aeschylus (in the *Oresteia*) and Sophocles (in his *Electra*). Euripides himself had already dramatized parts of this mythic complex in *Electra* (probably around 420 BCE) and *Iphigenia among the Taurians* (written ca. 414 BCE), and he returned to it again soon after *Orestes* in *Iphigenia in Aulis* (produced posthumously after 406 BCE). But the specific story presented here has no parallels in any surviving tragedy and is likely to have been invented by Euripides. All of the characters and some of the elements of the plot— Orestes' trial for murdering his mother, Menelaus' return from Troy after the death of Agamemnon, the comradeship between Orestes and Pylades, Apollo's intervention to help Orestes, and the divinization of Helen—are perfectly traditional; but Euripides has integrated them into a thoroughly novel plot full of twists and surprises. His exploration of the tumultuous relationships involving Orestes, Electra, and Pylades is likewise highly original, while his deployment near the end of a singing Phrygian in place of the usual speaking messenger to report (confusingly) on the events in the palace, and the final scene with actors at three levels of elevation (stage, roof, and "machine") provide some of the most sensational and spectacular moments in all of ancient theater.

Transmission and Reception

The evidence of quotations and allusions among later authors and the survival of at least twenty-four papyri containing fragments of the play (more than for any other Greek tragedy except Euripides' *Phoenician Women*) indicate that *Orestes* was extremely popular throughout antiquity. One remarkable papyrus, now in

Vienna, dates from about 200 BCE and preserves parts of lines 338-44 with musical notation. An inscription reports that the tragedy was successfully performed again at Athens in 341/40 BCE, with the famous actor Neoptolemus playing the title role. Further evidence for the play's continuing vitality on ancient stages may be the numerous interpolations in the text that have been detected by scholars, at least some of which may have been due to expansion by directors or actors. It seems too that Euripides' representation of Orestes' madness and hallucinations became almost proverbial. As for the play's critical reception in antiquity, some ancient scholars remarked that the play had a "rather comic turn of events," presumably in the sense that its plot turned out happily, and they noted that it was among the most celebrated plays on the stage. But they also complained that its characters were inappropriately bad, since all except Pylades were quite wicked. Already in the fourth century BCE Aristotle had criticized Euripides for having made Menelaus' character even worse than his plot required.

Orestes not only was selected as one of the ten canonical plays most studied and read in antiquity, but also, together with *Hecuba* and *The Phoenician Women*, became one of the three plays of the so-called Byzantine triad. As a result, it is transmitted in hundreds of medieval manuscripts and is equipped with very full ancient and medieval commentaries. But for the most part it does not seem to have left much of a trace on ancient pictorial art, with the exception of a striking wall painting in Ephesus from the second century CE, depicting two actors playing the roles of Electra and Orestes in the opening scene of the play, with Orestes lying on his sickbed.

The popularity of *Orestes* in the Greek Middle Ages continued during the Renaissance in the West. But by the end of the eighteenth century its fortunes had already begun to decline. The increasing popularity of Aeschylus' *Oresteia* and Sophocles' *Electra* meant that for over two centuries their canonical versions have tended to eclipse Euripides' more eccentric one. Since the mid-twentieth century, however, the play's elements of political nihilism, its extreme mood swings, and its peculiar mixture of high and low examples of human behavior, as well as its musicality and bold stage effects, have attracted a resurgence of stage productions, adaptations, and critical interest. One provocative revival of the play was that by Jan Kott (1968). Other productions of note (some of them quite heavily adapted) were directed by Alexis Solomos (1971), John Barton (1981), and Emma Gersche (2009). Adaptations of the play have been also been written by Adrienne Kennedy (1972), Tadashi Suzuki (1983), Charles Mee (1992), and Nancy Meckler (1986, 2006), and by now it ranks once again among the most staged—but still also as one of the most disconcerting—of all of Euripides' dramas.

ORESTES

Characters   ELECTRA, sister of Orestes; daughter of
Clytemnestra
HELEN, wife of Menelaus
HERMIONE, daughter of Menelaus and Helen
CHORUS of women of Argos
ORESTES, brother of Electra; son of
Clytemnestra
MENELAUS, husband of Helen
TYNDAREUS, king of Sparta; father of Helen
and Clytemnestra
PYLADES, friend of Orestes
MESSENGER
PHRYGIAN SLAVE
APOLLO

*Scene: In front of the palace of Agamemnon in Argos. Near the door,
huddled under blankets on a pallet, lies Orestes asleep. Electra is
sitting next to him.*

ELECTRA
  There is no form of anguish with a name—
  no suffering, no fate, no fall
  inflicted by heaven, however terrible—
  whose burden human nature could not bear.
  Tantalus, the son—they say—of Zeus himself,   5
  and blessed by birth and luck, now writhes and trembles
  in terror of the rock that overhangs his head,

though even as a man he sat as honored equal
at the table of the gods, but could not hold his tongue,   10
being sick with pride.
                    Or so at least they say.
The son of Tantalus in turn was Pelops,
father of Atreus for whom the weaving Fates
wove the threads of strife, a war with his own brother,
Thyestes.
          But why should I linger on the horrors
of my house?
          Atreus feasted him on his murdered sons.°   15
I pass over in silence the intervening years.
Atreus with Aerope fathered two sons,
Menelaus and famous Agamemnon—
if what he had was fame.
                    The wife of Menelaus
was Helen, whom the gods in heaven themselves
despise, while Agamemnon married Clytemnestra   20
in a marriage that was noted throughout Greece.
By her he had three daughters—me, Electra,
and my two sisters, Chrysothemis and Iphigenia—
and one son, Orestes there. All of us his children
by that one mother, wickedest of women,
who snared her husband in the meshes of a net   25
and murdered him.
                    I leave it to the world
to consider her motive. It is no topic for a maiden
like myself.
          And why repeat the old charges
against Apollo?
                    The world knows all too well
how he pushed Orestes on to murder the mother
who gave him birth, an act not everyone   30
approved. But persuaded by the god, he killed,
and I did what a woman could to help him,

while Pylades, our friend, shared the deed
with us.°

        After the murder Orestes collapsed   35
to bed. There he lies, wasted by raging fever
and whirled on to madness by his mother's blood—
I dare not breathe the name of those Eumenides°
who pursue him now, hounding him with terror.
Six days have passed now since our mother's murder,
and since her body was purified in the pyre.   40
And all that time he has not tasted food
or bathed himself, but there he lies instead,
huddled in the blankets. When the fever lifts,
he turns lucid and cries; then suddenly, madly,
bolts from the bed like an untamed colt.   45
Meanwhile Argos has declared us matricides
and outlaws, forbidding anyone to speak to us
or give us shelter.

                But this day decides our fate.
On this day the city gathers in assembly
to vote on whether we two shall live or die,   50
and, if we die, then by stoning or the sword.°

              One single hope is left.
Our uncle Menelaus has just come home
from Troy. His fleet fills the harbor at Nauplia,
riding at anchor just offshore after all those years
out of Troy.

             But Helen—the cause of so much grief—   55
he was so terrified that she might be seen
and stoned by the fathers of those who died at Troy,
that Menelaus sent her on ahead last night
under cover of darkness.

            She is here now,   60
inside the house, weeping over her sister's death
and the ruin of our house.

             She has as comfort

for her woes her unwed daughter, Hermione,
whom Menelaus, before he sailed for Troy,
brought from Sparta and entrusted to my mother's care.   65
In her she finds some solace, and can forget
her troubles. Now I watch the roads in hope
of seeing Menelaus on his way.
Unless he helps us now, then we must die,
for we are strengthless. Nothing is so weak
and helpless as a fallen house.   70

> (Enter Helen from the palace, carrying a pitcher
> for libations and a lock of her own hair.)

HELEN

       There you are.
Oh, dear Electra, Clytemnestra's daughter . . .
But you poor girl, still not married!
And how are you, dear?
       And how is poor Orestes?
To murder his own mother! But for my part
I can see no reason on earth for shunning you.   75
The real culprit was Apollo.
       And yet, poor sister,
Clytemnestra! To think I sailed for Troy
on that tragic voyage without even seeing her!
Some god must have driven me mad.
       And now she is gone,
and I am left to mourn for her misfortune!   80

ELECTRA

Why tell you, Helen, what you can see for yourself?
There lies the wreck of Agamemnon's son,
while I sit here at my sleepless post
beside his corpse. But for a little breath,
a corpse is what he is.
       I do not complain   85
on his account.

                    But you, so fortunate, you and your husband both,
        you come to us now in our utter misery.

HELEN

        When did he collapse in bed like this?

ELECTRA

                    On the day
        he spilt his mother's blood.

HELEN

                    Poor man, and oh! Poor mother,   90
        for how she died.

ELECTRA

                    Indeed, that's how things stand:
        so he collapsed.

HELEN

                    I wanted to ask, niece,
        could you do me a favor?

ELECTRA

                    Only if I can:
        you see I'm busy sitting by my brother.

HELEN

        Would you go for me to my sister's grave?   95

ELECTRA

        What?
                    You want *me* to go to my mother's grave?
        But why?

HELEN

                    To pour libations on her grave
        and leave this little clipping of my hair.

ELECTRA

        But she was *your* sister. You should go yourself.

HELEN

        I am afraid, ashamed to show my face
        in Argos.

ELECTRA

This repentance comes a little late.
Where was your shame when you ran away from home
and left your husband?

HELEN

Spoken with more truth than kindness.   100

ELECTRA

Why are you ashamed to face the Myceneans?

HELEN

The fathers of those who died fighting at Troy—
they frighten me.

ELECTRA

They should. You're quite a byword
here in Argos.

HELEN

Please go. Save me from this fear.

ELECTRA

I could not bear the sight of my mother's grave.   105

HELEN

But it wouldn't do to send a servant there.

ELECTRA

Then send Hermione.

HELEN

Send an unmarried girl
on an errand in public?

ELECTRA

It is her duty.
She owes it to my mother for bringing her up.

HELEN

Quite right, my dear.

I'll follow your advice.° 110
Yes, I'll call her out. An excellent suggestion!

(Helen calls into the palace.)

Hermione, dear, please come outside the house.

(Enter Hermione from the palace.)

Take this libation and these clippings of hair
and go to Clytemnestra's grave. Stand there 115
and pour this mixture of honey, milk, and wine
over the grave and, as you pour, repeat these words:
　　　　　"Your loving sister Helen,
prevented by her fear of the Argives from coming
to your grave in person, sends you these gifts."
Then implore her to be gracious to us all,
to you, my husband, me, and these poor children 120
whom a god has destroyed. Promise her besides
that I will labor to perform, like a good sister,
all the dues and rites of the gods below.
Now go, dear. Hurry there, make your offering
and then come back as quickly as you can. 125

(Exit Hermione with offerings to the side, Helen into the palace.)

ELECTRA
Oh, what a vileness beauty is in humans,
and yet salvation for those whose nature's fine!°
Did you see how she clipped the merest tips of her curls,
so stingy with her loveliness?
　　　　　The same old Helen!
O gods, how can you help loathing this woman, 130
who has completely ruined my brother and me
and all Hellas?

(Enter the Chorus of Argive women from the side.)

　　　　　But here they come again,
those loving friends who sing in lamentation
with me.

Now if they wake him from his sleep,
if I must see my brother going mad   135
once more, I shall cry out my eyes with grief.

(To Chorus.)

Walk softly, friends. Gently!
                 Hush.
Quiet, quiet. Not a step or sound.
Your kindness is well meant, of course, but still
it will be a great misfortune if you wake him.°

CHORUS [*singing in this lyric interchange with Electra, who sings in response*]
Hush.

STROPHE A
Not a sound. Tiptoe softly.°   140
Barely, barely touch the ground.

ELECTRA
Back, back from the bed!

CHORUS
Back we go.

ELECTRA
                 Your music, friends—
keep it down, flute it low,   145
as soft as gentle breath may go
down the stem of your reed.

CHORUS
There. Hear it, so soft,
so low.

ELECTRA
                 Yes, just like that.
Now tiptoe to me, softly, so,
and tell me why you come   150
now that he sleeps at last,
he sleeps.

CHORUS

How now? How?
Will he live? Will he die?

ELECTRA

He breathes, he breathes—
but his breath comes slow.   155

CHORUS

                    What?
The wretched man!

ELECTRA

                    If you wake
his sleeping eyes, you kill him!
He is enjoying sweet sleep
at last.

CHORUS

                    Condemned to suffer   160
for a god's command!
How terribly he suffers!

ELECTRA

Evil the act, evil the god,
that evil day Apollo on his throne
commanded my mother's death,   165
murder for murder!

CHORUS

                    STROPHE B
Look, look!
In the bed—his body stirring!

ELECTRA

Yes, your cries have wakened him,
have broken his sleep!

CHORUS
>No, no.
He sleeps, he sleeps.

ELECTRA
>Back,
back from the bed.
>Not a sound,   170
not a cry.
>For god's sake, go!

CHORUS
Now he sleeps.

ELECTRA
>Then let him sleep.
O Night, mother of mercy,°
blessed night,
who gives to human anguish   175
the lovely gift of sleep,
rise,
>rise from your abyss
and soar to Agamemnon's house,
where all is ruin,
>all is loss!   180
>Hush.
>No more.
In the name of god, be still,
be still! No more mourning,
or you rob him of his peace,
this gracious peace of sleep!   185

CHORUS
>ANTISTROPHE B
Where, where will it end?

ELECTRA
Death, death.

What is left
but death? He refuses food.

CHORUS
Then death must come.   190

ELECTRA
     Yes,
Apollo has sacrificed us both,
giving bloody vengeance for our mother,
the murderer of our father!

CHORUS
The revenge was just.

ELECTRA
     But terrible!
O mother who gave me birth,
who killed and was killed,   195
you slew your husband,
you killed your children too.
By your death we died.
We are the living dead.   200
This man is dust and ashes,
while I, a living ghost,
dead to this sunlit world,
stalk with withered life,
childless, unmarried,   205
crying my sorrow, lost,
alone in the endless night.

CHORUS LEADER
Electra! Look and see if your brother has died
while we were mourning. He lies so still now—   210
I do not like it.

(Orestes wakes.)

ORESTES

> O sweet wizard sleep,
> savior of the sick, dear loveliness
> that came to me in my worst need of you!
> O goddess sleep, goddess of forgetting,
> to whom the unhappy make their prayers,
> how skilled, how wise!
>
> But what happened?
> Who put me here?
> I somehow—can't remember.   215

ELECTRA

> How happy it made me to see you fall asleep
> at last.
>
> Should I raise you up, my dear?

ORESTES

> Yes, please. Help me up.
>
> Now wipe away
> this crust of froth around my mouth and eyes.   220

ELECTRA

> This service is sweet, and I do it gladly,
> nursing my brother with a sister's love.

ORESTES

> Sit here
> beside me. Now brush this matted hair
> from my eyes so I can see.

ELECTRA

> Oh, that poor head!
> And your hair, all snarled and dirty! You're so wild   225
> and unwashed!

ORESTES

> Let me lie back down.

That's better. After these attacks of fever,
my arms and legs seem somehow limp.

ELECTRA

Lie down
and don't move. Sick men must stay in bed.
Frustrating, I know, but it can't be helped.   230

ORESTES

Prop me up again. Now turn me around.
What nuisances we sick are in our helplessness!

ELECTRA

Would you like to try walking a step or two?
The change may do you good.

ORESTES

With all my heart.
Right now even the suggestion of health,   235
however false, would be welcome.

ELECTRA

Listen, Orestes,
I have something to say. But you must listen now
while your mind is clear and the Furies leave you free.

ORESTES

If your news is good news, by all means tell me.
If not, I have troubles enough.   240

ELECTRA

Listen then.
Our uncle Menelaus is here, in Argos.
His fleet lies at anchor at Nauplia.

ORESTES

What?
Is it true? Then this darkness has a dawn?
Our uncle here? The man for whom our father
did so much?

ELECTRA

          Here in person—trust my words—   245
and Helen too. He has brought her home from Troy.

ORESTES

  I'd envy him more if he'd survived alone.
If his wife is here, he has brought his trouble home.

ELECTRA

  Poor Tyndareus.

          What daughters he fathered!°
And both disgraced him in the eyes of Hellas.   250

ORESTES

  Take care that you act differently: *you* can.
I mean purity of heart as well as word.

                        (Orestes starts to behave wildly.)

ELECTRA

  Orestes!

          O gods, your eyes are whirling!
Oh no! No!

          Help! He is going mad!

ORESTES

  No, Mother!

          For god's sake, Mother,   255
keep them away, those bitches with bloodshot eyes,
those writhing snakes!

          Help! They're coming,
they're leaping at me!

ELECTRA

          Please, go back to bed.
You don't see what you think you see.

ORESTES

  Apollo, save me!

          They want to kill me,   260

those bitches with Gorgon eyes, those goddesses
of hell!

ELECTRA

I won't let you go. I'll hold you with my arms
and stop you from this wild jumping!

(She grasps Orestes around his waist.)

ORESTES

Let me go!
I know *you*. You're one of my Furies too!
You're holding me down to hurl me into hell!   265

(He breaks loose and springs up.)

ELECTRA

What can I do?
How can I help him now?
There's nothing human that can save us. No,
heaven hates us both.

ORESTES [*speaking to an imagined attendant*]
Get me my horn-tipped bow,
the bow Apollo gave me to scare these bitches off   270
if they threatened me with madness.

(He shoots from an imaginary bow.)

Vanish, demons!
Goddesses you may be, but unless you go,
this human hand shall draw your blood.
Damn it, go!
Ignore me, do you?
Don't you see this bow
already drawn, this arrow already flying?
What? Still here?
Vanish, spread your wings!   275
Skim the air, will you! Go hound Apollo,
accuse his oracle. But go! Go!

(He returns to sanity.)

What was I saying?
        And why am I panting so?
What am I doing here, out of bed?
        But wait—
I remember now—a great storm, the waves crashing—
but now this calm—this peace.

(To Electra.)

        Why are you crying?   280
Why do you hide your face?
        Oh, my poor sister,
how wrong it is that what I have to suffer,
this sickness, this madness, should hurt you too
and cause you trouble.
        Please, dear, please don't cry,
not on my account.
Let me bear the burden.
I know, you consented to the murder too,
but I killed, not you.
        No—
I accuse Apollo. The god is the guilty one.   285
It was he who drove me to this dreadful crime,
he and his words, egging me, encouraging me,
all words, no action.
        I think now
if I had asked my dead father at the time
if I should kill her, he would have begged me,
gone down on his knees before me, and pleaded,   290
implored me not to take my mother's life.
Her death could never bring him back to life
and I, by killing her, would have to suffer
as I suffer now.
        It seems so hopeless, dear,
I know.

But lift your head; do not cry.   295
And sometimes when you see me morbid and depressed,
comfort me and calm me, and I in turn,
when you despair, will counsel you with love.
In families there is no better way,
for each to help the other.
                    Now go inside.   *For love is all we have, the*   300
Bathe and eat and give those tired eyes *only way that each can help*
the sleep they need. If you too should collapse, *the other.*
if you fall ill yourself from nursing me,
then I am dead. You are my only help;   *— I need her!*   305
there's no one else.

ELECTRA
                    I could never leave you.
Live or die, I live or die with you, Orestes.
For you are my hope too, as I am yours.
What am I without you?
                    A woman,
brotherless, fatherless, friendless, alone
and helpless.
                    But since you think it best, dear,   310
I'll go inside.
                    But you go back to bed
and rest. Above all else, try to stay calm
and master your terror, if you can. Remember:
no getting out of bed.
                    A sickness may be real
or something in the mind, but in either case,
a person still feels exhaustion, pain, despair.   315

             (Exit Electra into the palace. Orestes returns to his bed.)

CHORUS [*singing*]
                    STROPHE

Goddesses of terror,
runners on the wind,

revelers of sorrow
whose rites are tears! 320
Women of darkness,
Eumenides whose wings
shiver the taut air,
demanding blood,
avengers of murder,
we implore you—
release this boy,
Agamemnon's son, 325
from madness of murder,
the blood that whirls him on!
Pity, pity we cry,
pity for the crime,
murder that came on,
drove from Apollo's throne,
the god's command to kill
breaking the hushed, the holy air,
with the word of blood—
spoken, spoken in the shrine 330
of Delphi—
Delphi,
holiest of holies
and navel of the world!

ANTISTROPHE

O Zeus, what mercy?
What mercy for this boy
for whom the struggle persists, 335
the spirit of vengeance
for his mother's blood,
savage spirit, dancing into his house
in gust on gust of grief,
blood and the madness of blood,
madness born of murder?
I mourn; I mourn.

Happiness is brief.
It will not stay. 340
God batters at its sails,
the tossing seas are wild;
anguish like a wind
whips down,
sorrow strikes,
swamps the scudding ship
and happiness goes down
and glory sinks.
        And yet
what other house, what name 345
more deserves our praise
than this line of glory,
born of Tantalus and Zeus?

              (Enter Menelaus from the side.)

[*chanting*]
And now behold the king—
royal Menelaus
whose magnificence declares 350
the blood of Tantalus!
All hail, the king!
Hail to the king who led
a thousand ships to Troy,
and did with heaven's help
all he vowed to do! 355
Hail him! Glory and success
go beside the king!

MENELAUS
Home from Troy at last.
        How happy I am
to see this house once more—
        but also sad,
for never have I seen a house more hedged about

by suffering than this.
                    I was putting in to shore
near Cape Malea when I first heard the news   360
of Agamemnon's murder at the hands of his wife.
For Glaucus, the god of sailors and a prophet
who does not lie, suddenly rose from the sea
in clear view, and he cried out:
                    "Menelaus,   365
your brother lies dying in his bath,
the last bath his wife will ever give him."
My crew and I alike burst into tears
at this dreadful news.
                    Well, so we reached Nauplia.
My wife Helen came on ahead at night,   370
and I was looking forward to seeing Orestes and his mother,
thinking, of course, that they at least were well,
when some sailor told me of the shocking murder
of Clytemnestra.
                    Can you tell me, women,   375
where I might find my nephew Orestes,
who brought himself to do this dreadful deed?
He was still a baby in his mother's arms
when I left for Troy, so I would not know him
if I saw him.

ORESTES

                    Here I am, Menelaus:
Orestes in person, and only too willing   380
to tell you the story of my sufferings.
But first I fall before you on my knees
and beg you, even without the suppliant's branch,
to rescue me from imminent disaster.
You come in the nick of time.

MENELAUS

                    Oh mighty gods,   385
is this some corpse I see?

ORESTES

More dead than living,
I admit. Still alive, but dead from all my troubles.

MENELAUS

And that wild, matted hair—how horrible you look!

ORESTES

It is my crimes, not my looks, that disfigure me.

MENELAUS

That awful stare—and those dry, cold eyes!

ORESTES

My body is dead. I am the name it had.   390

MENELAUS

But I did not expect this—alteration.

ORESTES

I am a murderer. I murdered my mother.

MENELAUS

So I have heard. Kindly spare me your horrors.

ORESTES

I spare you—although no god spared me.

MENELAUS

What is your sickness?

ORESTES

I call it conscience,   395
the certainty that I've committed evil.

MENELAUS

You speak somewhat obscurely. What do you mean?

ORESTES

I mean remorse. I am sick with remorse . . .

MENELAUS

A harsh goddess, I know. But there are cures.

ORESTES

   ...and madness too. The vengeance of my mother's blood.   400

MENELAUS

   When did this madness start?

ORESTES

           The very day
   we built her tomb. My poor mother's tomb!

MENELAUS

   Were you indoors or by the funeral pyre?

ORESTES

   I was outdoors by the pyre to gather her ashes.

MENELAUS

   Was there anyone there who could help you?   405

ORESTES

   Pylades. My accomplice in the murder.

MENELAUS

   But these phantoms. Can you describe them?

ORESTES

   I seemed to see three women, black as night.

MENELAUS

   I know them but I will not speak their name.

ORESTES

   Yes, they are dreadful. Naming them is uncouth.   410

MENELAUS

   So it's they who madden you for murdering your mother?

ORESTES

   Oh, if you knew the torture, how they're hounding me!

MENELAUS

   That criminals should suffer is hardly strange.

ORESTES

There is one recourse left.

MENELAUS

Suicide, you mean?   415
Most unwise.

ORESTES

No, not that. I mean Apollo.
It was he who commanded my mother's murder.

MENELAUS

A callous, unjust, and immoral order.

ORESTES

We obey the gods—whatever the gods may be.

MENELAUS

Apollo, despite all this, refuses to help?

ORESTES

Oh, he will. In his own good time, of course.   420
Gods are slow by nature.

MENELAUS

How long has it been
since your mother's death?

ORESTES

Six days now.
Her pyre is still warm.

MENELAUS

How quick they've been,
your mother's avengers coming after you!

ORESTES

Any man who acts ignobly to his friends
isn't truly wise.°

MENELAUS

        Well, what then of your father?   425
Is there any help from him?

ORESTES

        Nothing yet.
And nothing yet means nothing ever.

MENELAUS

How do you stand with the city?

ORESTES

        So hated
and despised that not one person in Argos
will speak to me.

MENELAUS

        Have your hands been cleansed
of the blood you shed?

ORESTES

        They shut their doors in my face.   430

MENELAUS

Who are your worst enemies in Argos?

ORESTES

        Oeax,
Palamedes' brother. He hated my father
because of what happened at Troy.

MENELAUS

        I see.
He wants your death in revenge for his brother.

ORESTES

Whom I never hurt. Three things really are killing me.

MENELAUS

Who else then? Friends of Aegisthus, I suppose?   435

ORESTES

    Yes, they all hate me, and the city gives them
    a hearing now.

MENELAUS

                But will they let you keep
    your father's scepter?

ORESTES

                Let me keep the scepter
    when they won't let me live?

MENELAUS

                What are their plans?

ORESTES

    The city is voting on our sentence today.   440

MENELAUS

    Exile from here? Or is it death or life?°

ORESTES

    Death by stoning.

MENELAUS

                Then why not try to escape?

ORESTES

    We are surrounded by a ring of bronze weapons.

MENELAUS

    Are they Argive soldiers? Or mercenaries
    hired by your enemies?

ORESTES

                It comes to this: 445
    everyone in Argos wants me dead.

MENELAUS

    Poor boy, you've reached the end.

ORESTES

                    And that is why
I turn to you.

                    You are now my only hope.
Menelaus, we are desperate. You, in contrast,
arrive in Argos at the moment of success.   450
I implore you: share that happiness with us,
your kin; don't hoard your power and success.
Help us.

                    Repay my father's services to you
by saving us.

                    For true friends show their love
in times of trouble, not just in happiness.   455

(Enter Tyndareus from the side, escorted by attendants.)

CHORUS LEADER
    Look:

                    aged Tyndareus of Sparta,
    he's hurrying here, his hair shorn close
    and dressed in black mourning for his daughter.

ORESTES
    Menelaus, this is the end for me. Here comes
    Tyndareus. Of all the men on earth,   460
    the one in whose presence I feel the deepest shame
    for what I did.

                    My grandfather, Tyndareus—
    the man who cared for me when I was small,
    who held me in his arms so tenderly—
    Agamemnon's baby boy—who loved me,
    he and Leda both, no less than their own sons,   465
    Castor and Polydeuces.

                    They loved me,
    and how have I returned their tenderness and love?
    O gods, this worthlessness I am!
    Where can I run?

What cloud can hide my face   470
from that old man's eye?

TYNDAREUS

Where can I find
my son-in-law Menelaus, women?
I was pouring libations on my daughter's grave
when I heard the news of his arrival home
at Nauplia after those long years abroad.
Helen is also here, I understand.
Can you show me the way?
I am most eager
to grasp his hand again after his long absence.   475

MENELAUS

Hello, old Tyndareus, who shared your wife with Zeus!

TYNDAREUS

Menelaus, my son!

(He sees Orestes.)

What?°
Look at him: the man who murdered his mother,
coiled like a snake at the door, those sick eyes
glowing like coals!
What a loathsome sight!   480
How can you bear to speak to such a monster?

MENELAUS

Why not? I loved my brother. This is his son.

TYNDAREUS

This, Agamemnon's son? A creature like *this*?

MENELAUS

His son, in trouble, and I honor him.

TYNDAREUS

Your foreigners, I see, have taught you their own ways.   485

MENELAUS

It is a Greek custom, I think, to honor your kin.

TYNDAREUS

But not to put yourself above the laws.

MENELAUS

Necessity is legislator here.
The wise say: under compulsion, no man's free.

TYNDAREUS

That is your view. It never will be mine.

MENELAUS

Your age—and anger—cripple your understanding.   490

TYNDAREUS

The man being tried for lack of understanding
is this one!°
        If right and wrong are clear to all,
what man ever acted with smaller understanding
of right and wrong than this man?
        Not once,
mind you, did he weigh the justice of his cause
or avail himself of the common law of Greece!   495
What should he have done?
        When his father died—
killed, I admit, by my own daughter's hand,
an atrocious crime which I do not condone
and never shall—he should have prosecuted
his mother, charged her formally with murder,   500
and made her pay the penalty prescribed,
expulsion from his house.
        Instead of disaster
he would have gained much fame for moderation,
sticking to the law and remaining pious.
        But now,
what difference is there between him and his mother?

No, she was vicious, he was right—and yet
the evil he has done by killing her   505
has far surpassed her crime.
                          Think again, Menelaus.
Suppose now this man's wife murders her husband.
Her son then follows suit by killing her,
and his son then must have his murder too
and so on.
                  Where can this chain of evils end?   510
No, our ancestors handled these matters well
by banning their murderers from public sight,
forbidding them to meet or speak to anyone.
But the point is this: they purged their guilt   515
by banishment, not death. And by so doing,
they stopped that endless vicious cycle
of murder and revenge.
                          Do not mistake me.
I despise adultery and unfaithful wives,
and my daughter, that husband-slayer, most of all.
As for your wife Helen, I loathe her too   520
and never wish to speak to her again.
Nor, I might add, do I envy you at all
that you went to Troy to get that evil woman.
No sir, not my daughters, but the law:
that is my concern. There I take my stand,
defending it with all my heart and strength
against the brutal and inhuman spirit of murder
that corrupts the cities and ruins this whole land.   525

                                        (To Orestes.)

You monster! Where was your pity, your humanity,
when your mother bared her breast and beseeched you
for her life?
                  I did not see that pitiful sight,
but the very thought of it makes the tears come
to these old eyes.

                    One proof I know for certain: 530
that heaven loathes you. These fits of madness
are the price you pay for murder; heaven itself
has made you mad. No further proof is needed.
So be warned, Menelaus.
                    If you help this man,   535
you challenge the express will of heaven.
So let him be. Let them stone him to death
or—I give you warning, sir—never set foot
in Sparta again.°
                    My own daughter is dead,
and she deserved to die, but it was wrong
that he should kill her.
                    Except for my daughters,   540
I might have lived a happy man and died in peace.
But there my fortunes failed.

CHORUS LEADER
                    Lucky that man
whose children are his happiness, and not
a notorious grief.

ORESTES
                    Sir, I shrink from speaking,
knowing almost anything I say will displease you   545
or offend you.°
                    My murder of my mother was,
I admit, a crime. But in another sense,
since, by killing her, I avenged my father,
there was no crime at all.
                    Wait. Listen.
Let me speak. This respect I feel for your age
cripples me, overawes me. If you only knew
how that white hair of yours harrows me   550
with shame.
                    What else could I have done?
I had two duties, two clear options,

both of them conflicting.
                    My father begot me,
my mother gave me birth. She was the furrow
in which his seed was sown. But without the father,°
there is no birth. That being so, I thought,   555
I ought to stand by him, the true agent
of my birth and being, rather than with her
who merely nourished me.
                    And then your daughter—
I blush with shame to call that woman my mother—
in a mock marriage went to a lover's bed.
I disgrace myself as much as I hurt her
by this admission. And yet I must admit it.   560
Aegisthus was her secret husband at home.°
And so I killed them both, first him, then her—
committing, indeed a very impious act,
but avenging my father.
                    For this you threaten me
with stoning. But, in fact, I did a service   565
for all of Greece.
                    For tell me, what would happen
if our women decided to adopt my mother's example,
killed their husbands and then came rushing home
to their children, exposing their breasts for pity?
Why, they could murder a man for any trifle,
on any pretext. But my "crime," as you call it,   570
has stopped that practice for good.
                    As for my mother,
I had every right to hate her and to kill her.
Her husband away from home, leading all Greece
in arms—what did she do? She took a lover   575
and betrayed his bed!
                    And when she saw she'd erred,
did she do the proper thing and punish herself?
No, not my mother. Instead, she murdered him
to save herself.

I should not invoke the gods
when defending myself on a charge of murder,
but in the name of the gods, if I'd accepted
her deed, what would that dead man have done to me?   580
Hounded me with the Furies of a father's hatred!
Or are there Furies on my mother's side,
but none to help him in his deeper hurt?
It was you: you destroyed me, Tyndareus.
You were the father of that woman who killed   585
my father and made a murderer of me.
And what of this?
     Odysseus had a son,°
but was Telemachus compelled to kill *his* mother?
No. And why? She refused to take a lover.   590
She was loyal to Odysseus.
     And what of this?
Have you forgotten Apollo, the god of Delphi,
navel and center of the world? The one god°
whose every oracle and word mankind obeys
blindly? He commanded my mother's murder.
Accuse him of murder, then. Put him to death.   595
He is the culprit, not I.
     What could I do?
Or was he competent to command a murder,
but now incompetent to purge the guilt?
Then where can I go, what can I do,
if the god who ordered me to kill my mother
cannot, or will not, save me?
     One more thing.
Let no man say that what we did was wrong,   600
but only that doing what we did, we did it
to our great cost and misery.
     As in action,°
so in marriage too. Marry, and with luck
it may go well. But when a marriage fails,
then those who marry live at home in hell.

CHORUS LEADER

Women by nature, it seems, were born to be   605
a great impediment and inconvenience
in the lives of men.

TYNDAREUS

             Since bluster is your answer,
since you insist on brazening it out
and every word you speak is said in spite,
I am even more impatient than before
to see you die.

             My purpose in coming here
was to lay some flowers on my daughter's grave.   610
But now, by god, I have a further motive —
your death!

             I will go to the assembly of the Argives.
I'll fire them up against you and your sister
until they vote to stone you both to death!
Yes, your sister too!

             She deserves it,   615
by god, even more than you do!

             It was she,
that girl, who incited you against your mother,
stuffing your ears day in and day out
with her malice, telling of Agamemnon's fate,
tattling to you of your mother's adultery —
which I dearly hope offends the gods below   620
as much as it disgusted us on earth!
That was her effort. Yes, she worked on you
until she set this whole house on fire
with the arson of her malice.

             One thing more,
Menelaus: I warn you, if my love or hate
matter to you at all, do not oppose the gods
by rescuing this man.

             No, let them stone him,°   625

or—mark my words—never set foot in Sparta
again.
　　　　　I warn you, do not make the mistake
of siding with outlaws and criminals like this
against god-fearing and law-abiding men.
Servants, lead me away.

(Exit Tyndareus to the side, escorted by attendants.)

ORESTES　　　　　　　　　　　*(To Tyndareus as he departs.)*
　　　　　Good. Go.　　　　　　　　　　　　　630
Let Menelaus hear the rest of my appeal
uninterrupted. Spare us the nuisance
of your senility.
　　　　　　　But, Menelaus,
why that troubled look? And why are you pacing
up and down that way?

MENELAUS
　　　　　Let me think.
I am trying to decide on the wisest course.　　　635
And, frankly, I am puzzled.

ORESTES
　　　　　　　Then postpone decision
for a while. Hear what I have to say
and then deliberate.

MENELAUS
　　　　　That's fair enough.
There are times for keeping still and times
for speaking out. This is the time to speak.
Go ahead.

ORESTES
　　　　　Forgive me if I speak at length.　　　640
Longer speeches can be more persuasive,
and better, than short ones.

Listen, Menelaus.
It's nothing of your own that I need now. What I want
back from you is what my father gave you once—
by which I don't mean possessions. I mean life.
Give me my life and you give me my most precious   645
possession.

           I committed a crime, and I admit it.
It's fair that you should wrong me in return.
When my father mustered an army for the siege
of Troy, he also did a wrong—and yet
that wrong was generous. He did that wrong for you,
to right the wrong that your wife Helen did.   650
And wrong for wrong, you owe me that wrong now,
Menelaus.

           Good brother that he was,
my father volunteered his life for you,
fighting as a soldier at your side.
And why? For this: to help you get your wife
and bring her home.

           What you had of him,   655
I now exact of you. Fight on my behalf,
not ten long years, but one brief day.
Again, my sister Iphigenia died at Aulis
on your account. But any claim I have on you
for my sister's death, I freely waive.
Hermione may live. For as things stand now,   660
I cannot press my claim, and I forgive you
your advantage.

           But repay my father's loan;
settle your score with him by saving me,
and my sister too, unwedded to this day.
Think: if I die, I leave my father's house
heirless, orphaned of life.

           Impossible,   665
you say?

           But surely this is just the point,

Menelaus.

        If you love us, this is the time
to help, now, when everything we have
is lost.

        Who needs help when the gods are good
and all is well? No, the man whom heaven helps
has friends enough. But now we need your help.

        All Hellas knows how much you love your wife.
I am not trying to flatter you or wheedle you,   670
but in Helen's name, I beg you—
        O poor me!
What I have come to! And yet I must endure
humiliation and make this supplication
in the name of all our house, our family,
O Uncle, my father's brother, save us now!
Imagine that my dead father in his grave   675
listens to me now, that his spirit is hovering
over you, that he himself is speaking, pleading
through my lips!
        You have seen our sufferings
and our despair, and I have begged you for my life—
life, the one hope of every man on earth,
not mine alone.

CHORUS LEADER

        I am only a woman,   680
but I implore you: help them, save them, please.
It's in your power.

MENELAUS

        Of course I honor you,
Orestes, and I want to share your troubles.
For we are joined by a common bond of blood,
and I am honor bound to help you out   685
when you're in trouble, if the gods will let me,
dying myself, and killing your enemies.°
But the power to help you only the gods can give.

And I've arrived in Argos in a weakened state—
devoid of support—my allies have dwindled away—
myself exhausted by my terrible ordeal.   690
So defeating Argos by a show of strength
is out of the question.

                Instead, our weapons must be
diplomacy and tact. Inadequate,
I admit, but not, perhaps, quite hopeless.
Whereas even to suggest the use of force°
as a way out, given our present weakness,
is folly.   695

           Mobs in a fury are like a fire,
it's dangerous to try to fight their rage.
Hands off is best. You sit quietly by,
watching and waiting, patiently biding your time
while their anger runs its course unchecked.
With any luck, it quickly burns itself out,
and in the lull, while the wind is shifting,   700
anything you want is yours for the asking.
Anger, however, is only one of their moods;°
pity is another—they're precious assets both,
if you know what you're doing.

              Now this is my plan.
I'll go and smooth matters over
with Tyndareus and the city and persuade them   705
to moderate their tone.

            As with sailing,
so with politics: make your cloth too taut,
and your ship will dip and keel, but slacken off
and trim your sails, and things head up again.
The gods, you know, resent being importuned
too much; in the same way the people dislike
being pushed or hustled. And our only chance
of saving you at all lies in skill and tact,   710
not in force, as you perhaps imagine.
I lack the men and strength your rescue requires;

and the Argives, I know, are not the sort of men
to be overawed by threats.°
                    No, if we're wise,
we will do what we must and accept the facts.   715
We have no other choice.

                              (*Exit Menelaus to the side.*)

ORESTES
                    You vile coward!
What in god's name have you ever done
but fight a war to bring your wife back home?
So now you turn your back and you desert me?
What Agamemnon did for you's forgotten?   720
My father, in trouble, was deserted by his friends.
And now my last hope, my only refuge
from death at the hands of the Argives has abandoned me.

                    (*Enter Pylades from the side, running.*)

But wait.
                    Look! I see Pylades,
my best friend, running here to me, on his way   725
from Phocis!
                    Thank god! What a sight!
A friend, a loyal friend, in my despair.
No sailor ever saw a calm more greedily
than I now see my friend!
                    Pylades!

PYLADES
I seem to have reached here none too soon, Orestes.
Coming through town, I heard that the Argives are meeting   730
and saw it myself. They're discussing some proposal
to execute your sister and you.
                    What's happening?
How are you doing, Orestes, dearest friend
and cousin and age-mate—you're all that to me!

ORESTES

To put it in a nutshell: we are ruined.

PYLADES

If that is so, include me in that "we."   735
Friends share and share alike.

ORESTES

That traitor Menelaus—
he betrayed my sister and me.

PYLADES

I am not surprised.
A vicious husband for a vicious wife.

ORESTES

By coming home
he helped my cause as much as if he'd stayed in Troy.

PYLADES

Then the rumor was true? He really has returned?

ORESTES

Somewhat late. His treachery, on the other hand,   740
was promptness itself.

PYLADES

What about that bitch Helen?
Did he bring her home?

ORESTES

No, the other way around.
She brought him.

PYLADES

Where is she hiding now?
Where is that woman who murdered so many Argives?

ORESTES

In my house—if I have any right to call it mine.

PYLADES

What did you ask Menelaus?

ORESTES

        To intercede for us   745
and save our lives.

PYLADES

        By god, what did he say to that?
This I want to hear.

ORESTES

        Oh, patience, caution, and so on.
What cowards say to friends.

PYLADES

        And his excuse?
That tells me everything.

ORESTES

        We were interrupted.
That old man came. You know the man I mean—   750
the father of those precious daughters.

PYLADES

        Tyndareus himself?
Furious with you, I suppose, because of your mother?

ORESTES

You've hit it. So Menelaus took the old man's side
against my father.

PYLADES

        He refused to help you at all?

ORESTES

Oh, he's no soldier—though he's quite the man
with the ladies.

PYLADES

        Then you really are in trouble.
Must you die?   755

ORESTES

              The citizens are trying us for murder.

PYLADES

What will their verdict be? I dread your answer.

ORESTES

Life or death—small words, but big in meaning.

PYLADES

Then leave your house, escape together with Electra.

ORESTES

Don't you see the sentries posted everywhere?   760

PYLADES

I saw armed men patrolling the streets.

ORESTES

              We are surrounded
like a city under siege.

PYLADES

              Ask what happened to me.
I have suffered too.

ORESTES

              Your troubles on top of mine?
What happened?

PYLADES

              My father Strophius banished me from Phocis.   765

ORESTES

Banished you? On his authority as your father?
Or did he take you to court on a formal indictment?

PYLADES

For aiding and abetting the murder of your mother—
that "shocking crime," as he calls it.

ORESTES

              Heaven help you,
if you must suffer on my account!

PYLADES

        I am no Menelaus.

I can take it.

ORESTES

        But aren't you afraid of the Argives?   770
Suppose they decide to put you to death with me?

PYLADES

They have no jurisdiction. I am a Phocian.

ORESTES

Don't be too certain. In the hands of vicious men,
a mob will do anything.

PYLADES

        But under good leaders
their counsels are always excellent.

ORESTES

        You're right.
So let's discuss together.

PYLADES

        What about?

ORESTES

Suppose, for instance, I went to the meeting myself   775
and told them . . .

PYLADES

        . . . that you were completely justified?

ORESTES

Yes, that I avenged my father.

PYLADES

        I doubt they'd be satisfied.

ORESTES

But what am I supposed to do? Sit here and sulk?
Die without saying a word in my own defense?

PYLADES

A coward's act.

ORESTES

Well, what then should I do?

PYLADES

Can you hope to survive by staying here?

ORESTES

No, not at all.

PYLADES

And if you go to the meeting?

ORESTES

Something might be gained.

PYLADES

Then, clearly, you have to go. 780

ORESTES

Good enough. I'll go.

PYLADES

You may be killed, of course,
but at least you'll die fighting.

ORESTES

And escape a coward's death.

PYLADES

Better than by staying here.

ORESTES

And my cause is just.

PYLADES

Pray heaven that it seem that way to them.

ORESTES

Besides, they may pity me . . .

PYLADES

     Yes, your high birth.

ORESTES

  . . . feeling indignation at my father's murder.   785

PYLADES

Then our course is clear.

ORESTES

     Absolutely. I must go.
I refuse to die a coward's death.

PYLADES

     Spoken like a man.

ORESTES

Wait. Should we tell Electra?

PYLADES

     Great heavens, no!

ORESTES

There'd probably be tears.

PYLADES

     Which wouldn't be auspicious.

ORESTES

Clearly silence is best.

PYLADES

     And will save no little time.

ORESTES

One strong objection still remains . . .

PYLADES

     What's that?   790

ORESTES

My madness, if I have an attack.

PYLADES

               Have no fear.
You are in my hands.

ORESTES

               Madmen are hard to handle.

PYLADES

I will manage.

ORESTES

               But if my madness strikes you too?

PYLADES

Forget it.

ORESTES

               You're certain then? You're not afraid?

PYLADES

Afraid? Fear in friendship is an ugly trait.

ORESTES

Then lead on, my helmsman . . .

PYLADES

               Love leads you. Follow me.   795

ORESTES

Take me first to my father's grave.

PYLADES

               What for?

ORESTES

To implore his help.

PYLADES

               Agreed. This pilgrimage is good.

ORESTES

But don't, for god's sake, let me see my mother's grave!

PYLADES

No. She hated you.
                But hurry. We must go now,
or the Argives may have voted before we arrive.
Here, lean yourself on me.
                Now let the people jeer!   800
I'll lead you through the city, proud and unashamed.
What is my friendship worth unless I prove it now
in your time of trouble?

ORESTES

                "Provide yourself with friends
as well as kin," they say. And the proverb tells the truth.
One loyal friend is worth ten thousand kinsmen.   805

                (*Exit Orestes and Pylades to the side.*)

CHORUS [*singing*]

             STROPHE

Where, where are they now—
that glister of golden pride,
glory that camped at Troy
beside the Simois,
the boast of happiness
blazoned through Hellas?
Back and back they ebb,   810
a glory decays,
the greatness goes
from the happy house of Atreus.
Beneath the proud facade
the stain was old already—
strife for a golden ram,
and the long stain spread
as the curse of blood began—
slaughter of little princes,   815
a table laid with horror,
a feast of murdered sons.

And still corruption swelled,
murder displacing murder,
as through the blooded years
the stain spread on in time
to reach at last
the two heirs of Atreus.

And what had seemed so right,
as soon as done, became
evil, monstrous, wrong!
A mother murdered—
her soft throat slashed 820
by the stabbing sword,
and the blade raised high
while the brandished blood
fell warm from the steel,
staining, defiling
the sun's immaculate light.
Damnable, awful crime!
Sacrilege of madness born!
In horror, in anguish,
before she died,
his mother screamed— 825
"No, no, my son, no!
Do not kill your mother
to revenge your father!
Do not make your life
an eternity of shame!" 830

What madness like this?
What terror, what grief
can compare with this?
Hands, hands of a son,
stained with mother's blood!
Horror too inhuman

for mortal mind to bear.
The man who slew his mother
murdered and went mad. 835
Raving Furies stalk him down,
his rolling eyes are wild—
mad eyes that saw
his mother bare her breast 840
over her cloth of gold—
saw, and seeing, stabbed,
avenging his father
with his mother's murder!

(Enter Electra from the palace.)

ELECTRA

But where is Orestes? For god's sake, women,
where did he go? Has he had another attack? 845

CHORUS LEADER

No, Electra. He went to the Argive meeting
to stand his trial and speak in his own defense.°
Upon what happens there your lives depend.

ELECTRA

But why? And who persuaded him?

CHORUS LEADER

          Pylades.
But I think I see a messenger on the way. 850
He can answer your questions.

(Enter Messenger from the side.)

MESSENGER

          Lady Electra,°
poor daughter of our old general Agamemnon,
I bring you bad news.

ELECTRA

          If your news is bad, 855

I hardly need to guess: we must die.
The sentence is death.

MESSENGER

Yes. The Argives have voted
that you and your brother must die today.

ELECTRA

Death!
But I expected no less. For a long time now
I dreaded in my heart that this would happen.   860
But what did they say? What were the arguments
that condemned us to death?

And how are we to die,
my brother and I? By being stoned to death   865
or by the sword?

MESSENGER

I happened to be coming,
madam, by chance, from the country into town,
thinking to get some news of how things stood
with you and Orestes. Your family, you see,
always took good care of me and, for my part,
I was grateful to your father to the end.
I may be only a poor peasant, ma'am,
but when it comes to loyalty, I'm as good   870
as any man.

Well then, I saw a crowd
go streaming up to take their seats on the hill—
the same place where they say that Danaus
held the first public meeting in Argos
when Aegyptus put him on trial.

But anyhow,
seeing all that crowd, I went up and asked,
"What's happening here? Is there a war?   875
What's all this excitement for?"

"Look down,"

says someone. "Don't you see Orestes there?
He's on his way to stand trial for his life."
Then I saw a sight I never saw before,
and one whose likes I never hope to see
again:
                    Orestes and Pylades together,   880
the one hunched down with sickness and despair,
the other sharing his troubles like a brother
and helping him along as though he were a child.
As soon as the seats were filled, a herald rose.
"Who wishes," he cried, "to speak to the question?   885
What is your wish? Should the matricide Orestes
live or die?"
                    Then Talthybius got up—
the same man who fought with your father at Troy.
But he spoke like the toady he always was:
a two-faced speech, compliments for your father   890
in contrast to Orestes, cheap malicious stuff
puffed out with rolling phrases. And the gist?
Orestes' example was dangerous for parents.
But, needless to say, he was all smiles and sweetness
for Aegisthus' cronies.
                    But that's your herald for you—°   895
always jumping for the winning side, the friend
of any man with influence or power.
                    After him
King Diomedes spoke. It was his opinion
that you both should be banished, not killed,
since this would be enough for piety's sake.   900
The response was mixed: some agreed with what he said;
others disapproved noisily.
                    The next to speak
was one of those cocky loudmouths, an Argive
but not really from Argos—if you take my meaning—
anybody's man—for a price, of course—
sure of himself and reckless in his bluster,   905

but glib enough to take his hearers in.°
He moved that Orestes and you should be stoned
to death, but in fact it was Tyndareus prompting him   915
as to what he ought to say.°
               But then at last
someone stood up to take the other side.
Nothing much to look at, but a real man;
not the sort one sees loafing in the market
or public places, ma'am, but a small farmer,
part of that class on which our country depends;   920
knowing how to argue closely when he wants,
an honest, decent, and god-fearing man,
beyond reproach.
              Now in this man's opinion,
Orestes deserved a crown. What had he done,
after all, but avenge his father's murder
by killing a godless, worthless, adulterous woman?   925
A woman, too, who was keeping men from war,
making them stay at home, tormented by the fear
that if they left, those who remained behind
would seduce their wives and destroy their families
and homes.
             His words convinced the better sort.   930
No one else spoke.
            So then Orestes rose.
"Men of Argos,"° he said, "it was for your sake
as much as for my father that I killed my mother.
For if you sanction this murder of husbands by wives,   935
you might as well go kill yourselves right now
or accept the domination of your women.
But you will not, you must not, do it.°
As things now stand, my father's unfaithful wife
is dead. But if you vote that I must die,   940
then the tradition of inherited norms and customs
must fall, and you are all as good as dead,
since wives will have the courage of their crimes."

In short, a well-framed speech, and yet he failed;
while that cheap blabber, by playing to the mob,
induced them to pass a sentence of death.   945
Poor Orestes was barely able to persuade them
not to stone him to death, and then only
by promising that you and he would kill yourselves
today.

        Pylades, in tears, is bringing him home   950
from the meeting, followed by a group of friends,
all weeping and mourning. Such is his return,
and a bitter sight it is.

        So prepare the noose,
or bring out the sword, for you must die
and leave the light. Neither your high birth
nor Apollo in his shrine at Delphi helped. No,   955
Phoebus has destroyed you both.

                          (Exit Messenger to the side.)

CHORUS LEADER
        Poor wretched girl.°
Look at her now, her head hung down,
dumb with grief, trembling on the verge of tears!

CHORUS° [*singing*]
                STROPHE

O country of Pelasgia,
let me lead the cry of mourning!   960
With white nails I furrow my cheeks,
beat my head,
each blow struck
for the queen of the dead,
goddess Persephone underground!
Mourn, you Cyclopean land!   965
Shear your hair, you virgins,
and raise the cry of pity,
pity for those who die,
who led the fighting men of Hellas!   970

Down and down, this house.
Pelops' line is ended,
the ancient happy house,
its envied greatness gone.
Envy and resentment
out of heaven struck.
Envy was the vote   975
the men of Argos took.
O generations of mortals,
tearful, toilsome mankind,
look, look on your hopes,
cut down with failure and crossed with death.
The passing generations go,
changing places, changing lives.   980
Human life passes understanding.

ELECTRA° [*singing*]
O gods in heaven, take me,
lift me to heaven's middle air
where the great rock,
shattered from Olympus,
swings and floats on golden chains!
Lift me, take me there
and let me cry my grief to Tantalus,   985
founder of my house,
father of my fathers,
the ruin of my house that I have seen—
the winged race
as Pelops' swerving car
spurred along the sea,
Myrtilus hurled in murder down,   990
the body tossed
from the hurtling car
where the boiling surf
pounds and batters on Geraestus!

And the curse drove on
and the stain of blood spread— 995
the sign appeared
in Hermes' flocks,°
a ram with golden fleece,
portending terror,
doom to Atreus, breeder of horses,° 1000
the quarrel in the blood
that drove the golden sun awry,
forced the glistering car
westward through the sky
where lonely Dawn drives down
her snow-white steeds.
And Zeus, in horror of that crime,° 1005
changed the paths
where the seven Pleiades turned and flared.
And still the spreading stain,
murder displacing murder,
betrayal and broken faith,
Thyestes' feast of horror
and the adulterous love
of cunning Aerope of Crete. 1010
And now the curse comes home,
the inescapable taint,
finding fulfillment at last
in my brother and me!

                    (Enter Orestes and Pylades from the side.)

CHORUS [*chanting*]
And here your brother comes
under his sentence of death.
And with him comes Pylades,
most loyal of his friends, 1015
guiding like a brother
poor Orestes' stumbling steps.

ELECTRA

    Orestes—

              O gods, to see you standing there,
    so close to death, the grave so near—
    I cannot bear it! I weep. To see you now   1020
    for the very last time! I'm going to lose my mind!

ORESTES

    Enough, Electra. No more of these womanish tears.
    Resign yourself. It is hard, I know,
    but you must accept our fate.°

ELECTRA

              How can I stop?   1025
    Look, look at this light, this gleaming air
    we shall never see again!

ORESTES

             No more, Electra.
    Isn't it enough that the Argives have killed me?
    Must you kill me too?

ELECTRA

             But you are so young,
    too young to die! You should live, Orestes! Live!   1030

ORESTES

    Don't make me weep! These lamentations of yours
    will make me a coward.

ELECTRA

             But I'm about to die!
    Life is sweet, sweet! No one wants to die.

ORESTES

    No, but we have no choice. Our time has come.   1035
    We merely have to choose the way in which we die:
    by the sword or the rope.

ELECTRA

     Kill me yourself then,
Orestes. Don't let some Argive disgrace
the daughter of Agamemnon.

ORESTES

     I have my mother's blood
upon my hands. I will not have yours too.   1040
Do it in any way you wish, but you must do it
yourself.

ELECTRA

     If I must, then I must. I'll stab myself
right after you do! But let me put my arms
around your neck.

ORESTES

     What is it worth,
this poor hollow pleasure—if those who are dying
have any pleasure left?

ELECTRA

     Oh, my brother,
dearest, sweetest name I know—my life!   1045

ORESTES

O gods, this breaks my heart—
     with all my love
I want to hold you too.
     What shame on earth
can touch me any more?
     Oh, my sister,°
these loving words, this last sweet embrace
is all that we shall ever know in life   1050
of marriage and children!

ELECTRA

     If only one sword

could kill us both! If we could only share
one coffin together!

ORESTES

Then death might be sweet.
But how little now of all our family is left   1055
to bury us!

ELECTRA

Menelaus said nothing to help?
He betrayed our father like the coward he is?

ORESTES

No, not once did he so much as show his face.
Not once. His eyes were glued upon the throne;
oh, he was careful not to help.
                              But come,
we must die as we were born—nobly,   1060
as the children and heirs of Agamemnon should.
I shall show the city of what blood I come
by falling on my sword. As for you,
follow my example and die bravely.
                              Pylades,
you please oversee our deaths; then lay us out   1065
when we are dead, and make us both one grave
beside my father's tomb.
                              And now, good-bye.
I go to do what must be done.

PYLADES

Wait!
Stop, Orestes. I have one reproach to make.
How could you think that I would want to live   1070
once you were dead?

ORESTES

Why should my dying
mean that you should die?

PYLADES

     You can ask me that?
How can I live when my only friend is dead?

ORESTES

       It was I who murdered my mother, not you.

PYLADES

We murdered together, and it is only just
that I share the cost with you.

ORESTES

     No,   1075
Pylades. Live; go home to your father.
You still have a country you can call your own;
I do not. You have your father's house
and you inherit wealth, great wealth.
That marriage with Electra which, as my friend,
I promised you, you've lost. But marry elsewhere;   1080
have children.
        The bonds which bound us once
are broken now. And now good-bye, my friend,
my best, my only friend.
        And so fare well.
Faring well at least is something you may have,
but I cannot. The dead have lost their joys.

PYLADES

How little you seem to understand, Orestes.   1085
If I desert you now to save myself,
may this green and growing earth refuse
my ashes, the golden air shelter me no more!
I murdered with you, and I affirm it
proudly. And it was I who planned that crime   1090
with you and her.
       Yes, with her, I said.
She is my wife, the wife you promised me.

What would my story be when I go home
to Delphi and Phocis?
                    That when all was well,   1095
I was your firm friend, but my friendship withered
when your luck ran out?
                    No, Orestes,
                    I have my duty too.
But since we have to die,
let us think and see if there is any way
of making Menelaus suffer too.

ORESTES

Let me see that sight and I could die   1100
content.

PYLADES

                    Then do what I ask you and wait now.

ORESTES

With pleasure, if only I can be revenged.

PYLADES   (*Indicating the Chorus.*)
Whisper. Those women there—I don't trust them.

ORESTES

They're all right. They're friends.

PYLADES

                    Then listen.
We'll murder Helen. That will touch   1105
Menelaus where it hurts.

ORESTES

                    But how?
If we can manage it, I'm more than willing.°

PYLADES

A sword in the throat. Unless I'm mistaken,
she's hiding in your house now.

ORESTES

        Oh yes,
and putting her seals on everything we own.

PYLADES

But not for long. Hades will be her new husband.

ORESTES

But how can we do it? She has a retinue   1110
of slaves.

PYLADES

        Slaves? Is that all she has?
I'm not afraid of any Phrygian slaves.

ORESTES

Creatures who manage her perfume and mirrors!

PYLADES

Gods! Did she bring those luxuries here from Troy?

ORESTES

Oh, Hellas is far too small to hold that woman now.

PYLADES

What are slaves worth in a fight with men   1115
who were born free?

ORESTES

        If we can bring this off,
I'll gladly die twice.

PYLADES

        And so would I,
to get revenge for you.

ORESTES

        But describe your plan.
Every step.

PYLADES

        First of all, we go inside
on the pretext of killing ourselves.

ORESTES

        Good enough.   1120
But then?

PYLADES

        Then we make a great show of tears
and tell her how much we suffer.

ORESTES

        At which, of course,
she'll burst into tears. But she'll be laughing inside.

PYLADES

Why then, so will we—exactly the same.

ORESTES

But how do we kill her?

PYLADES

        We'll carry swords   1125
hidden in our robes.

ORESTES

        But what about her slaves?
Should we kill them first?

PYLADES

        No, we'll lock them up
in different rooms.

ORESTES

        But if they scream for help,
then we'll kill them.

PYLADES

        And once we're through with them,
the way is clear. Right?

ORESTES

Death to Helen! 1130
That will be our motto.

PYLADES

Now you have it.
But observe the beauty of my plan.

First,
if we killed a better woman than Helen,
it would be outrageous murder.

This is not.
No, we punish her in the name of all Hellas
whose fathers and sons she murdered, whose wives 1135
she widowed.

Mark my words, Orestes.
There will be bonfires and celebrations in Argos;
men will call down blessings on our heads,
thank us, congratulate us for doing away
with a vicious, worthless woman. No longer 1140
shall they call you "the man who murdered his mother."
No, a fairer title awaits you now,
the better name of "the killer of Helen
who killed so many men."

And why, in god's name,
should Menelaus prosper when you, your sister,
and your father have to die?—I omit your mother 1145
with good reason. If, through Agamemnon,
Menelaus has his wife, he shall not, must not,
have your house.

For my part, let me die
if I do not lift my sword against that woman!
But should we fail, should she escape our hands,
we'll burn this house around us as we die! 1150
One way or another, Orestes, we shall not be cheated
of glory.

Honor is ours if we die;
fame, if we escape.

CHORUS LEADER
                    Every woman
justly loathes the name of Helen, the woman
who disgraced our sex.

ORESTES
                    Nothing in this world   1155
is better than a friend. For one true friend
I would not take in trade either power or money
or all the people of Argos. It was you,
my best friend, who planned our murder of Aegisthus.
You shared the risks with me, and once again,
good friend, you give me my revenge   1160
and all your help.

                    But I say no more,
lest I embarrass you by praising you
too much.

                    I have to die. Very well then,
but above all else I want my death
to hurt the people I hate. They betrayed me,   1165
they made me suffer, so let them suffer now
for what they did to me.

                    Am I or am I not
the son of Agamemnon, the man who ruled
all Hellas, not as a tyrant, but by his merits,
with godlike power?

                    And I shall not shame him
by dying like a slave. No, I die free,
and I shall have my free revenge on you,   1170
Menelaus!

                    That revenge alone
would make me happy. If—which I doubt—
we could murder Helen and then escape,

so much the better. But this is a dream,
a prayer, a futile hope. It cheers the heart,
but nothing more.

ELECTRA

Orestes, I have the answer!
A way out for us all!

ORESTES

That would take a god.
But where is this answer? I ask you because
I know your intelligence.

ELECTRA

Listen then. You too, Pylades.

ORESTES

Go on. Good news would make pleasant hearing now.

ELECTRA

Do you remember Helen's daughter, Hermione?

ORESTES

That little girl our mother took care of?

ELECTRA

Yes.
She has gone just now to Clytemnestra's tomb.

ORESTES

What for? And what if she has?

ELECTRA

She went
to pour libations for her mother's sake.

ORESTES

And so?
What does this have to do with our escape?

ELECTRA

Seize her as a hostage when she comes back.

ORESTES
What good will that do us three?

ELECTRA
Listen, Orestes.   1190
Once Helen is dead, Menelaus may attempt
to hurt one of us three—you or him or me—
though it hardly matters who: we are all one here.
Well, let him try. You merely set your sword
at Hermione's throat and warn him you will kill her
at the first false move. If then, seeing Helen   1195
lying in a pool of blood,° he decides he wants
his daughter's life at least and agrees to spare you,
let the girl go. On the other hand,
if he tries to kill you in a frantic burst of rage,
you slit the girl's throat. He may bluster   1200
in the beginning, but he'll soon see reason,
I think. The man's a coward, as you know:
he won't fight.
                        And there you have my plan
for our survival. That's it.

ORESTES
What a woman!
The mind of a man with a woman's loveliness!   1205
If ever a woman deserved to live, not die,
that woman is you.
                        What do you say now,
Pylades? Will you forfeit a woman like this
by dying, or will you live, marry her,
and be happy?

PYLADES
Nothing would please me more.
My dearest wish is to go home to Phocis
with Electra as my bride.

ORESTES

Electra, I like your plan   1210
in every respect—provided we can catch
the traitor's cub. How soon, do you think,
will Hermione return?

ELECTRA

Any moment now.
The length of time at least is right.

ORESTES

Perfect.   1215
Electra, you stay here outside the house
and wait for her. Watch out too in case someone,
especially an ally or brother of her father,°
gets into the house before the murder's done: 1220
beat with your fist on the door or raise a cry,
to let us know.

You and I, Pylades—
I know I can count on your help now, my friend—°
will go inside, get our swords and make ready
to settle our final score.

O you my father,   1225
ghost who walks the house of blackest night,
your son Orestes calls upon your help
in his hour of need! It is for you, Father,°
I suffer. For you I was condemned to death
unjustly! And your own brother has betrayed me,
though what I did was right. Come, Father,
help me to capture his wife! Help me kill her!   1230
O Father, help us now!

ELECTRA

O my father,
if you can hear our prayers beneath the earth,
come, rise in answer! We are dying for you!

PYLADES

O Agamemnon, kinsman of my father,
hear my prayers!
                    Help us! Save your children!

ORESTES

I murdered my mother...

PYLADES

                    I held the sword that killed!   1235

ELECTRA

I encouraged him! I made him brave!

ORESTES

...helping you, father!

ELECTRA

                    I didn't betray you either.

PYLADES

Hear our reproaches and save your children now!

ORESTES

I offer my tears to you.

ELECTRA

                    And I my grief.

PYLADES

Enough.
                    We must be about our business now.   1240
If prayers can penetrate this earth below,
he hears.
                    —O Zeus, Zeus of our fathers,
great power of justice, help us now,
help us to victory!
                    Three friends together,
one common cause, one trial,
and together we shall live or die!°   1245

(Exit Orestes and Pylades into the palace.)

ELECTRA [*alternately singing and speaking in this lyric exchange with the Chorus, who sing in reply*]

STROPHE

Women of Mycenae,
noble women of Argos, one word with you, please.

CHORUS°

What is it, my lady? For you
are mistress still in the city of Argos.   1250

ELECTRA [*speaking*]

I want half of you to watch the highway.
The rest of you will stand guard over here.

CHORUS

But why this task, lady?
Tell me, my dear.

ELECTRA [*singing*]

A premonition. I am afraid   1255
someone might see my brother about to kill
and cause us new grief on top of old grief.

(The Chorus divides into two sections.)

FIRST HALF-CHORUS LEADER [*speaking here and throughout*]

Come on now, women, hurry! To your posts!
I'll watch the road to the east.

SECOND HALF-CHORUS LEADER [*speaking here and throughout*]

And I'll watch here   1260
on the westward side.

CHORUS

We are turning our eyes to one side
and the other, just as you say.   1265

ELECTRA
ANTISTROPHE
Whirl your eyes around
on every side; through your flying hair look all around you.

FIRST HALF-CHORUS [*singing here and throughout*]
Someone is coming! Look—a peasant
approaching the palace.

ELECTRA [*speaking*]
        Then this is the end.   1270
He'll betray our ambush to our enemies.

FIRST HALF-CHORUS
No. A false alarm. The road is empty.
There's no one there.

ELECTRA [*singing*]
        You on the other side,
is all well? Is there anyone in sight?   1275

SECOND HALF-CHORUS LEADER
All's well here. You watch there.
Not an Argive in sight anywhere here.

FIRST HALF-CHORUS LEADER
Nor here either. Not a soul in sight.   1280

ELECTRA
Wait then. I'll go and listen at the door.

CHORUS
Why is all quiet?
        Why this delay?
For god's sake, spill the victim's blood!   1285

ELECTRA [*speaking*]
EPODE
They do not hear us. O gods, what has happened?
Has her loveliness blunted their swords?

CHORUS

In a few minutes some Argive will be here
to rescue her, rushing up with drawn sword!   1290

ELECTRA

Look sharper than ever. No time for napping now!
Some of you turn to this way, some to that.

CHORUS

I'm moving along the path and looking everywhere.   1295

HELEN   *(From within.)*

Help me, Argos! Help! They'll murder me!

ELECTRA

Did you hear her scream? They're killing her!
That shriek! I'm sure that that was Helen screaming!

CHORUS

O Zeus, Zeus, send strength!   1300
Come, O Zeus! Help my friends now!

HELEN   *(From within.)*

Help me, Menelaus! Help! I'm dying!

ELECTRA AND CHORUS [*singing together*]
Murder!
        Butcher!
                Kill!
Thrust your twin swords home!
Slash, now slash again!
Run the traitress through,
kill the whore who killed   1305
so many brave young Greeks
by the spear beside the river,
those for whom we mourn,
by the waters of Scamander!   1310

CHORUS LEADER
Wait! Silence!

I hear the sound of footsteps.
Someone is coming.

ELECTRA [now speaking]

Here is Hermione
at the very moment of murder!

But not a sound.

Here she comes—walking straight for our trap,   1315
and a sweet catch she is, if I can take her.
Quick, back to your posts.

Seem natural
and unconcerned; don't give us away.
I had better have a sullen sort of look,
as though nothing had happened here.   1320

                    (Enter Hermione from the side.)

                              Ah,
have you been to Clytemnestra's grave, dear?
Did you wreathe it with flowers and pour libations?

HERMIONE

Yes, I gave her all the dues of the dead.
But, you know, I was frightened coming home.
I thought I heard a scream in the distance.   1325

ELECTRA

                              A cry?

Really? But surely we have every right
to cry a little.

HERMIONE

                    Not more trouble, Electra?
What has happened now?

ELECTRA

                    Orestes and I
have been sentenced to death.

HERMIONE

        God forbid!
You, my own cousins, must die?

ELECTRA

               We must.
This is necessity whose yoke we bear.   1330

HERMIONE

Then that was why I heard that cry?

ELECTRA

                    Yes.
He went and fell at Helen's knees . . .

HERMIONE

               Who went?
I don't understand.

ELECTRA

        . . . Orestes, to implore Helen
to save our lives.

HERMIONE

        Then well might the palace   1335
have rung with your cries.

ELECTRA

            What better reason
could there be?
        But if you love us, dear,
go now, fall at your mother's feet
and beg her, implore her by her happiness
to intercede with Menelaus now
on our behalf. My mother nursed you in her arms: 1340
have pity on us now and save our lives.
Go plead with her. You are our last hope.
I will take you there myself.

HERMIONE

      Oh yes, yes!

I will go quickly! If it lies in my power,   1345
you are saved.

(Exit Hermione into the palace. Electra follows her to the door.)

ELECTRA

       For god's sake, Orestes,
Pylades! Lift your swords and seize your prey!

HERMIONE   *(From within.)*

Who are these men?
          Help!
          Save me!

ELECTRA°

       Silence,
girl.
     You are here to save us, not yourself.
Hold her, seize her!
        Put your sword to her throat   1350
and bide your time.
        Let Menelaus learn
with whom he has to deal now. Show him
what it means to fight with men, not cowards
from Troy. Make him suffer for his crimes!

(Exit Electra into the palace.)

CHORUS [*singing*]

STROPHE

—*Quick, raise a shout!*
     —*A cry!*
—*Drown the sound of murder in the palace!*
—*A shout, before the Argives hear*   1355
  and come running to the rescue!
—*Before they come, first let me see*
  Helen, dead for sure, lying in her blood,
  or hear the story from one of her slaves.
—*Something has happened; but what I do not know.*   1360

—God's vengeance on Helen,
  justice crashing from heaven!
            —Justice for Helen
            who made all Hellas mourn,
            mourn for her lover's sake—
—For Paris, bitter curse of Ida,   1365
  Paris, who led all Hellas to Troy!

                    (Enter Phrygian Slave, running, from the palace.)

CHORUS LEADER
  Hush. Be still.
            The bolts on the great doors
  are sliding—a Phrygian is coming out—
  someone who can tell us what has happened.

PHRYGIAN [*singing*]
  The Argive sword I've fled,
  from death I've escaped
            on barbarian slippers
  past the bedroom's cedar chambers   1370
  and the Doric triglyphs,
  gone, gone, Earth, Earth,
  with barbarian runnings!
  Oh, oh.
            Where can I run, foreign ladies?   1375
  Fly up to the white air?
  Or to the sea the godbull Ocean cradles,
  circling the world?

CHORUS LEADER
  What is it, man of Ida, Helen's slave?   1380

PHRYGIAN
  Oh, oh,
            Ilium, Ilium, Troy, Troy!
            Holy hill of Ida!
  Hear the barbarian dirge I cry,°   1385

death by Helenbeauty brought,
eye of doom,
of birdborn loveliness the eye,
Helen from Hell, Helen from Hell!
Leda's puppy, Fury
that broke Apollo's burnished walls of Troy!   1390
Otototoi!
Pity, pity, I cry
for ill-fated Troy and for Ganymede,
ravished to bed
by Zeus the rider!

CHORUS LEADER
Tell us clearly what has happened indoors.
For what you've said so far bewilders me.°

PHRYGIAN
Ailinos!   1395
      Ailinos!
the dirge begins,
the dirge we barbarians cry in Asian voices
for royal blood and princes dead
by murderous iron sword!
            Ai ai!
      I tell you all.
            Into the palace came   1400
a pride of lions, Greeks, twins.
One was the son of a general;
the other, Pylades, man of plots, evil;
just like Odysseus, a silent cheater,
but loyal to friends, and bold,   1405
skilled for war, a killer-snake.
God damn him dead
for his cool plotting of evil!
Once they're in they make for the throne
of bowman Paris' wife,   1410
sobbing tears smeared everywhere.

Oh so humble, they sit down,
one on the left, one on the right,
put their hands on the lady's knee,
begging life.
The Phrygian attendants were scared,   1415
came running, jumping, jumping.
One said, "Hey, treachery!"
"Look out, lady!" someone cried.
"No no," guessed other slaves,
but some were thinking,
                    "Hey,   1420
that snake who killed his mother
has tangled lady Helen
in cunning hunting nets."

CHORUS LEADER
And where were you? Or had you run away?   1425

PHRYGIAN
No, no, no.
                    In Phrygian fashion   1430
with foreign fan of feathers, yes,
I was fanning the hair of lady Helen,
rippling the air, the air to and fro,
gently over her cheek.
And while I fan,
                    slow, slow,
Helen's fingers wind the flax.
Spindle turning, fingers moving,
round and round flax on the floor,
Trojan spoils for a cloth of purple,   1435
a gift, yes, for Clytemnestra's tomb.
                    Orestes speaks to the Laconian woman:
"Deign, O madam, child of Zeus,
to place your feet on the ground,
come away from the dais, please.
Stand by ancient Pelops' hearth,   1440

hear what I have to say, please."
So he led her, led her, she followed,
poor suspecting nothing Helen.
Meanwhile, yes, his evil friend,
his Phocian partner in crime,°   1445
was doing other work.
                    "Go, go somewhere else!" he shouted,
 "you Phrygian cowards!"
Oh, and then he locked them up,
some in stables, others in colonnades,
some here, some there,
all of them from lady Helen barred away!   1450

CHORUS LEADER
And then what happened? Go on.

PHRYGIAN
O Mother of Ida! O mother!
Mighty, mighty! Oh, oh!
What I saw, I saw, in the house of princes!
Bloody sufferings, lawless evils!
                    Out of hiding,   1455
out of purple cloaks
they drew their swords!
And their eyes! Oh, spinning round
to look for danger anywhere.   1460
And then they came.
                    Like savage mountain boars
standing in front of the woman,
they shouted,
                "Die! Die!
Die for your traitor husband, that coward
who betrayed his brother's son,
who left him to die in Argos!"
She screamed, screamed out,
                "Ah, ah!"   1465
snow-white arms flailing, flailing,

beating bosom, beating head!°
Then in sandals golden
she leaped to run!
        But after her, after,
came Orestes on stout Mycenaean boots,
        caught her, oh,   1470
winding fingers in her hair
and neck forced back,
        down, down,
against the shoulder,
lifted, ah, sword to strike her throat!

CHORUS LEADER

But where were the Phrygian slaves? Couldn't you help?

PHRYGIAN

Oh, we shouted, yes!
        We battered doors
with iron bars, broke down panels   1475
where we were!
        Then we ran
to rescue her! From here, from there! Some with stones,
others with bows, with swords.
        But then!
Pylades came on—unflinching
like Phrygian Hector or Ajax with his triple helms   1480
(I saw him once at Priam's gates).
Steel on steel together met,
but soon we saw:
Phrygian men are no match for Greek ones.°   1485
        One ran, one dead,
this one wounded, and that one begging for his life.
So quick, quick, we ran, we hid!
Falling some, dying others,
staggering one with wounds.
And then, oh!

         Hermione came in
just as her poor mother was sinking to die.
The men, like Bacchants°
catching their wild prey on the mountain,
yet with no thyrsos in hand,
they snatched the girl, then turned back
again to kill Zeus' daughter.
But then, oh then—
suddenly, ah, ah!
she had vanished from the house,
O Zeus! O Earth! O Day! O Night!
as if by some magic drugs
or sorcerer's tricks or thieving gods!
What happened then I do not know.
No, no, run, I ran!
But Menelaus—
all his suffering, all his hurt
to bring the lady Helen home from Troy,
ah ah,
        all in vain.

        (Enter Orestes from the palace, his sword drawn.)

CHORUS LEADER
  On and on, one strangeness after another.
  And here's Orestes rushing from the palace
  with drawn sword!

ORESTES
        Where is that coward slave
  who ran from my sword inside?

PHRYGIAN [*speaking henceforth*]
        I bow down, my lord,
  I kiss the ground. It's Eastern custom, sir.

ORESTES
  This is Argos, fool, not Troy.

PHRYGIAN

But anywhere
wise men want to live, not die.

ORESTES

And those screams of yours?
Admit it: you were shouting to Menelaus for help. 1510

PHRYGIAN

Oh no, sir. Not I. For you I was screaming.
You need more help than he.

ORESTES

Did Helen deserve to die?

PHRYGIAN

Oh, yes sir. Three times cut madam's throat,
and I won't object.

ORESTES

This is cowardly flattery.
You don't believe it.

PHRYGIAN

Oh sir, I believe, sure.
Helen ruined Hellas, yes, killed the Phrygians too. 1515

ORESTES

Swear you're telling me the truth or I'll kill you.

PHRYGIAN

Oh, oh! By my life I swear—my highest oath!

ORESTES

Were all the Phrygians as terrified by cold steel
at Troy as you?

PHRYGIAN

Ooh, please, please, not so close!
All shiny murderous!

ORESTES

           What are you afraid of, fool?
Is it some Gorgon's head to turn you into stone?   1520

PHRYGIAN

Not stone—a corpse! But this Gorgon thing
I do not know.

ORESTES

           What? Nothing but a slave
and afraid to die? Death might end your suffering.

PHRYGIAN

Slave man, free man, everybody likes to live.

ORESTES

Well spoken. Your wit saves you. Now get inside.

PHRYGIAN

You will not kill me?

ORESTES

           I spare you.

PHRYGIAN

           Oh, thank you, thank you.   1525

ORESTES

Go, or I'll change my plan.

PHRYGIAN

           I don't thank you for that.

(Exit the Phrygian to the side.)

ORESTES

Fool, did you think I'd dirty my sword on your neck?
Neither man nor woman—who could want your life?
No, I came to stop your frightened screams. This city
of Argos is quickly roused to arms by any cry   1530
for help.

Not that I'm afraid of Menelaus either.
No, let him come. His glory is his golden curls,
not his sword.
But if he brings the Argives here
and in revenge for Helen's death refuses his help
to my sister, my friend and helper, and myself,   1535
then his daughter too shall join his wife in death.

(Exit Orestes into the palace.)

CHORUS° [*singing*]

ANTISTROPHE

O gods! Fate!
Grief comes down once more
upon the house of Atreus!
What should we do? Send to the city for help,
or keep silent?
Silence is the safer course.   1540
Look! Look up there on the roof—the smoke
pouring, billowing up!
And the glare of torches!
They are burning the house, the ancestral house!
They shrink from nothing!
God works his way with man.   1545
The end is as god wills.
Great too is the power of the fiends of vengeance,
blood for blood, against this house,
in vengeance for Myrtilus!

(Enter Menelaus with armed attendants from the side.)

CHORUS LEADER

Wait. I see Menelaus coming this way
in great haste. He must have heard some news
of what has happened here.
Stand your guard,   1550
inside the house! Quick, bolt the palace doors.
Beware, Orestes.

This man in his hour of triumph
is dangerous. Take care.

                    I have come
to investigate a tale of incredible crimes   1555
committed by two lions—I cannot bring myself
to call them men.
                    I am also told that Helen
is not dead, but has disappeared, vanished
into thin air, the idiotic fiction
of a man whose mind was almost crazed with fear
or, more probably, as I suspect, the invention
of the matricide and patently absurd.   1560
Inside there, open the doors!

                                        (The doors remain closed.)

                    Very well.
Men, break down that door so I can rescue
my poor daughter from the hands of these murderers
and recover Helen's body.°
                    In revenge for her,   1565
I personally shall put these men to death.

                    (Orestes, Pylades, and Electra appear on the roof of the
                        palace holding Hermione, a sword at her throat.)

ORESTES
You there, don't lay a finger on that door.
Yes, I mean *you*, Menelaus, you braggart!
Touch that door and I'll rip the parapet
from this crumbling masonry and smash your skull.   1570
The doors have been bolted down with iron bars
on purpose to keep you out.

MENELAUS
                    Gods in heaven!
Torches blazing—and people standing on the roof

like a city under siege, and—*no!*
A man holding a sword at my daughter's throat!   1575

ORESTES

Do you want me to ask the questions, Menelaus,
or would you prefer that I do the talking?

MENELAUS

Neither.
But I suppose I must listen.

ORESTES

                        For your information,
I am about to kill your daughter.

MENELAUS

                        Her too?
Wasn't it enough that you murdered her mother?

ORESTES

No, heaven stole her and robbed me of the pleasure.   1580

MENELAUS

This is mockery. Do you deny you killed her?

ORESTES

It pains me to deny it. Would to god I had . . .

MENELAUS

Had what? This suspense is torture.

ORESTES

                        . . . killed her,
struck down the whore who pollutes our land.

MENELAUS

Let me have her body. Let me bury her.   1585

ORESTES

Ask the gods for her carcass. In the meanwhile
I will kill your daughter.

MENELAUS

        The mother-killer°
murders again!

ORESTES

        His father's avenger,
betrayed by you.

MENELAUS

        Wasn't your mother's blood enough?

ORESTES

I can never have my fill of killing whores.   1590

MENELAUS

But you, Pylades! Are you his partner
in this murder too?

ORESTES

        His silence says he is.
But I speak for him.

MENELAUS

        Unless you fly away,
you will regret this act.

ORESTES

        We won't run away.
In fact, we'll burn the house.

MENELAUS

        Burn the house!   1595
Burn the palace of your fathers?

ORESTES

        To keep it from you.
But your daughter dies. First the sword,
then the fire.

MENELAUS

        Kill her. I shall get revenge.

ORESTES
  Very well.

MENELAUS
            No, wait! For god's sake, no!°

ORESTES
  Silence. You suffer justly for what you did.

MENELAUS
  Can justice let you live?

ORESTES
            Live—and reign too!   1600

MENELAUS
  Reign where?

ORESTES
            Here in Argos.

MENELAUS
  You?
  You officiate as priest?

ORESTES
            And why not?

MENELAUS
  Or sacrifice for war?

ORESTES
            If you can, I can too.

MENELAUS
  My hands are clean.

ORESTES
            Your hands, yes, but not your heart.

MENELAUS
  Who would speak to you?

ORESTES

        Those who love their fathers. 1605

MENELAUS

And those who love their mothers?

ORESTES

        Were born lucky.

MENELAUS

That leaves you out.

ORESTES

        Yes. I loathe whores.

MENELAUS

        Keep that sword away from my daughter!

ORESTES

        You're a liar,°

traitor.

MENELAUS

        Could you kill my child?

ORESTES

        Ah, the truth

at last!

MENELAUS

    What do you want?

ORESTES

        Persuade the people ... 1610

MENELAUS

Persuade them of what?

ORESTES

        ... to let us live.

MENELAUS

Or you will kill my child?

ORESTES

        It comes to that.

MENELAUS

  O gods, my poor wife ...

ORESTES

        No pity for me?

MENELAUS

  ... brought home to die!

ORESTES

        Would to god she had!

MENELAUS

  All my countless labors ...

ORESTES

        Nothing done for me.   1615

MENELAUS

  All I suffered ...

ORESTES

        Because you wouldn't help me.

MENELAUS

  I am trapped.

ORESTES

        Trapped by your own viciousness.
All right, Electra, set the house on fire!
You there, Pylades, most loyal of my friends,
burn the roof! Set these parapets   1620
to blazing!

MENELAUS

        Help, help, people of Danaus,
knights of Argos!

> To arms! To arms!
> This man with mother's blood upon his hands
> threatens our city, our very lives!

(*Apollo appears together with Helen above the palace.*)

APOLLO

> Stop. 1625
> Menelaus. Calm your anger.
> It is I,
> a god, Phoebus Apollo, son of Leto, who speak.
> You too, Orestes, standing there
> with drawn sword over that girl, hear
> what I say.
> Helen is here with me—
> yes, that same Helen whom you tried to kill 1630
> out of hatred for Menelaus. This is she°
> whom you see enfolded in the gleaming air,
> delivered from death. You did not kill her.
> For I, so commanded by Zeus the father,
> snatched her from your sword.
> Helen lives,
> for being born of Zeus, she could not die, 1635
> and now, between the Dioscuri in the swathe
> of air, she sits enthroned forever, a savior
> for sailors.
> Menelaus must marry again,°
> since the gods by means of Helen's loveliness
> drove Phrygians and Greeks together in war 1640
> and made them die, that earth might be lightened
> of her heavy burden of humanity.
> So much for Helen.
> I now turn to you,
> Orestes.
> It is your destiny to leave this land
> and go in exile to Parrhasia for a year. 1645

Henceforth that region shall be named for you,
called Oresteion by the Arcadians and Azanians.°
From there you must go to the city of Athena
and render justice for your mother's murder
to the three Eumenides.

                              Gods shall be your judges,   1650
sitting in holy session on the hill of Ares,
and acquitting you by sacred verdict.

                                          Then,
Orestes, you shall marry Hermione,
the girl against whose throat your sword now lies.
Neoptolemus hopes to make her his wife,   1655
but never shall, for he is doomed to die
when he comes to Delphi seeking justice
from me for his father's death.

                              Give Electra in marriage
to Pylades as you promised. Great happiness
awaits him.

                      Let Orestes reign in Argos,   1660
Menelaus. But go yourself and be king in Sparta,
the dowry of Helen, whose only dowry so far
has been your anguish and suffering.

                                I myself
shall reconcile the city of Argos to Orestes,
for it was I who commanded his mother's murder.   1665
I compelled him to kill.

ORESTES

                    Hail, Apollo,
for your prophetic oracles! True prophet,
not false!

                  And yet, when I heard you speak,
I worried I was hearing the whispers of some fiend
speaking through your mouth.

                    But all is well,   1670
and I obey.

See, I now release Hermione,
and we shall marry when her father gives
his blessing and consent.

MENELAUS

Farewell, Helen,
daughter of Zeus! You're blessed in your home
and happiness among the gods.
                    Orestes,   1675
I now betroth my only child to you,
as Apollo commands.
                    We come of noble birth,
you and I: may this marriage bless us both.

APOLLO

Let each one go to his appointed place.
Now let your quarrels end.

MENELAUS

                    I obey, lord.

ORESTES

And I. Menelaus, I accept our truce   1680
and make my peace with Apollo and his oracle.

APOLLO [chanting]

Let each one go his way.
Go and honor Peace,
loveliest of goddesses.
Helen I now lead
to the halls of Zeus,
upon the road that turns
among the blazing stars.   1685
There with Hera she shall sit,
with Heracles and Hebe throned,
a goddess forever,
forever adored—
there between her brothers,

the sons of Zeus,
reigning on the seas,
a light to sailors.

CHORUS [*chanting*]
  Hail, O Victory!°
  Preserve my life
  and let me wear the crown!

(All exit.)

TEXTUAL NOTES

(Line numbers are in some cases only approximate.)

HELEN

5: Some scholars reject the words "at home in Pharos, king in Egypt" as an interpolation.

9-10: The words "(because his father showed / the gods love in his lifetime" are partly unmetrical in the Greek and are rejected by many scholars.

85-89: Some scholars reject these lines (from "But tell") as an interpolation.

121-22: Some scholars reject these lines.

170-72: The text of these lines is uncertain.

175: The text and exact meaning of these words are uncertain.

181-82: The text of these lines is uncertain.

185: One or two words are missing here.

188: Several words are incorrectly transmitted in the manuscripts here.

235-37: Many scholars reject the words "he came / for my ill-starred beauty, / to capture my love" as an interpolation.

239: After this word, the manuscripts add "the sons of Priam"; this is rejected by most scholars as an interpolation.

257-59: Most scholars reject these lines.

287-92: Many scholars think these lines are an interpolation.

298-302: Many scholars reject these lines as an interpolation; in addition, line 302 is corrupt in part.

324-26: Some scholars reject these lines as an interpolation.

352: The words "and where was the story not clear?" are not properly preserved in the Greek.

365: The words "pain / on pain, tears upon tears, suffering" are unmetrical and the proper reading is uncertain in the Greek.

379: The text and exact meaning of these words are uncertain.

388–89: The words translated here "when you were constrained to make / an offering to the gods" are incoherent in the Greek, and many scholars reject them as an interpolation.

416: The words "could not ask" and "my ragged state" correspond to one line in the Greek that is rejected by many scholars as an interpolation.

441: The text and exact meaning of these words are uncertain.

448: The text of the middle part of this line is uncertain.

503–9: Some scholars reject these lines as an interpolation.

530–40: Some scholars reject these lines too.

556: The word "tomb" is a widely accepted modern emendation for the transmitted "place."

561: This line is not transmitted in the manuscript of this play but it has been restored to this location by scholars on the basis of a parody of this passage in Aristophanes' *Women at the Thesmophoria*.

625–97: The exact distribution of lines in this duet between Helen and Menelaus is uncertain and controversial.

637: The text of this line is uncertain.

669: One word is missing in the Greek but the meaning of the line is clear.

670: The words "and of Maia" have been added by scholars to repair the defective meter of this line.

679: The exact text of this line is uncertain.

690: In the manuscript these words are followed by a word meaning "shame" or "dishonor," which is rejected by editors as an interpolation.

704–5: The words from "We had" to "You mean" are rejected by many scholars.

713–19: Some scholars reject these lines as an interpolation.

728–33: Some scholars reject these lines too.

746-48: Many scholars reject these lines too.

752-57: Many scholars reject some or all of these lines too as an interpolation.

780: This verse is also transmitted as line 972 of Euripides' *Phoenician Women* and is rejected here by many scholars.

892-93: Many scholars reject these lines as an interpolation.

905-8: The text and meaning of line 905 are uncertain, and many scholars reject all four lines.

912-14: Many scholars reject these lines as an interpolation.

936: This word is corrupt in the manuscript.

991-95: Many scholars reject some or all of these lines as an interpolation.

1008: Some scholars reject this line too.

1131: The text of this line is extremely uncertain.

1149-50: The text and exact meaning of these lines are uncertain.

1157: Text and exact meaning of this line too are uncertain.

1162: Text and exact meaning uncertain.

1197: Some scholars reject this line as an interpolation.

1225: The last part of this line is corrupt and of uncertain meaning.

1226-30: Something has clearly gone wrong in the transmission of this passage. Different editors put these lines into different sequences, and some have suggested that at least two lines may be missing.

1227: "Be fooled" is a plausible modern emendation for the manuscript's nonsensical "die."

1279: Some scholars suggest that a line may be missing after this verse.

1286: Some scholars suggest that two half-lines may be missing after this word.

1313-14: The text here is uncertain; one or two words seem to be missing.

1318: A whole line seems to be missing here.

1326: Again, a line seems to be missing here.

1344: These words in the Greek make no sense; the correct reading is uncertain.

1353–54: These lines too are hopelessly corrupt and their sense is quite uncertain.

1366–68: Text and meaning very uncertain.

1374: Part of this line seems not to be correctly preserved.

1387: Many scholars have suggested that one or more lines may have been lost after this verse.

1422: The text and meaning of this line are quite uncertain.

1447–48: Text and meaning uncertain.

1451–53: The text of the opening lines of this strophe is very uncertain.

1472–76: The text of these lines is uncertain though their meaning is not in dispute; after line 1476 a whole line seems to be missing.

1512: This unmetrical line is rejected by editors as a patchwork, composed by someone much later than Euripides, that was meant to substitute for one or more genuine lines that had been lost.

1535: The text of most of this line is hopelessly confused and the meaning is uncertain.

1563–64: Text uncertain.

1650–55: Many scholars reject some or all of these lines as an interpolation; some transpose them to after line 1646.

1667–68: Some scholars delete the words "with the two sons of Zeus" and "have your libations" as an interpolation.

1679: The end of line 1679 does not make sense in the manuscripts; some scholars delete lines 1678–79 as an interpolation.

1682–83: Some scholars invert the order of these two lines.

1685: The text of this line is uncertain.

1688–92: Many scholars delete these lines, which are found at the end of a number of Euripides' tragedies, here and elsewhere, as an interpolation.

THE PHOENICIAN WOMEN

1–2: These lines are missing in ancient papyri of the play and are rejected by most scholars as an interpolation.

11: Many scholars reject this line too.

26-27: Many scholars reject both of these lines, or only the second one, as an interpolation.

51-52: Many scholars reject one or both of these lines; one ancient papyrus omits the second line.

118: Some scholars reject this line as an interpolation.

122-24: Some scholars reject these lines too.

132: Some scholars reject this line too.

141-44: Some scholars reject these lines as well.

175-77: The text of these lines is very uncertain.

185-89: The text of these lines is very uncertain.

291-92: These lines are missing in an ancient papyrus of the play and are rejected by many scholars.

301-3: The text of these lines is very uncertain.

344: This word is rejected by many scholars as an interpolation.

375-78: According to the ancient commentaries, the first of these lines was not found in some manuscripts; it and the following lines are rejected, all or in part, by many scholars.

387: This line is missing in an ancient papyrus of the play and is rejected by many scholars as an interpolation.

428: This line is criticized in the ancient commentaries as being superfluous and is rejected by many scholars.

436: This line is missing in an ancient papyrus of the play and is rejected by many scholars.

438-42: Many scholars reject these lines as an interpolation.

448-51: Some scholars reject these lines too.

478-80: Many scholars reject some or all of these lines as an interpolation.

520: Some scholars reject this line as an interpolation.

538: For this word, some manuscripts read "lawful."

548: Some scholars reject this line as an interpolation.

555-58: Many scholars reject these lines too.

566-67: Some scholars reject the second line, some both lines, as an interpolation.

623, 624: It is uncertain whether these two phrases should be assigned to Polynices or to Eteocles.

630: These words seem to be repeated from line 627 and may have displaced the original text; the whole line is rejected by some scholars.

645-50: The text and meaning of these lines are very uncertain.

667: The text of the last two words is uncertain.

679-80: The text of these lines is very uncertain.

690-96: Many scholars reject some or all of these lines as an interpolation.

697: This word is corrupt.

710-11: The text of these two lines is uncertain.

754-65: Many scholars reject some or all of these lines as an interpolation.

774-77: Some scholars reject these lines too.

781: The last part of this sentence is missing in an ancient papyrus and is rejected by some scholars.

790: The text of the last several words is uncertain.

792-93: Text uncertain.

800: The text of the last words is uncertain.

815-17: The text of the end of this antistrophe is extremely uncertain, and is also missing a few words.

847: This is a plausible scholarly emendation of the manuscript reading, "Every mule-cart."

868-80: Many scholars reject some or all of these lines as an interpolation.

882: This is a plausible scholarly emendation of the manuscript reading, "shafts."

886-90: Many scholars reject some or all of these lines.

944-46: Some scholars reject some or all of these lines.

973-74: The ancient commentaries criticize the second line as superfluous; many modern scholars reject that one or both lines.

990: Most of the manuscripts assign this line to Creon; many modern editors give it to Menoeceus instead.

1013–18: Many scholars reject some or all of these lines as an interpolation.

1070–71: Some scholars reject one or both lines.

1075: Some scholars reject this line too.

1101: Many scholars reject this line as well.

1104–40: Many scholars reject some or all of these lines too.

1183–85: Many scholars reject these lines.

1199: The last sentence is missing in many manuscripts and is rejected by many scholars as an interpolation.

1200–1201: Many scholars reject these lines as well.

1221–58: Many scholars reject these lines as an interpolation.

1262–63: Many scholars reject these lines too.

1265–69: Many scholars reject some or all of these lines.

1279: It is uncertain whether this line is spoken by Jocasta to Antigone or by Antigone to the Messenger.

1281: After this line most manuscripts transmit a verse which is identical with line 976 and is rejected here by most scholars.

1304: This is a plausible scholarly emendation of the manuscript reading, "light."

1308–53: This scene may have been rewritten for a later production; many scholars reject most or all of it as non-Euripidean.

1354–55: The manuscripts assign these lines to Creon; most modern scholars give them to the Chorus Leader instead.

1362: Most scholars reject this line as an interpolation.

1369–71: Many scholars reject these lines too.

1376: This line is identical with line 756 and is rejected here by most scholars.

1388–89: Most scholars reject these lines as well.

1396: After this word the manuscripts transmit some additional words that are corrupt; their text and meaning are very uncertain.

1429-30: The text of the end of the first line is uncertain; the second line is rejected by many scholars as an interpolation.

1463-65: Many scholars reject some or all of these lines as an interpolation.

1514: This line is corrupt and its meaning is uncertain.

1534: The text of this line is uncertain but its general meaning is clear.

1570-76: Some scholars reject these lines as an interpolation.

1582-1766: This last part of the play may have been rewritten for a later production; many scholars reject most or all of it as non-Euripidean.

1758-63: Most scholars reject these lines as an interpolation.

1764-66: These lines are also found at the end of *Hippolytus*, *Iphigenia among the Taurians*, and *Orestes*, and are rejected by most scholars as an interpolation.

ORESTES

15: This line is rejected by many scholars as an interpolation.

33: This line too is rejected by some scholars as an interpolation.

38: Text uncertain.

51: This line is rejected by many scholars.

110: This line is rejected by some scholars.

127: This line is missing in one manuscript and is rejected by most scholars as an interpolation.

139: This line is rejected by some scholars as an interpolation.

140-41: Some ancient sources, and some modern scholars, assign these lines not to the chorus but to Electra.

174-86: Some manuscripts assign some or all of these lines not to Electra but to the chorus.

249: Text uncertain.

422-24: At least two lines seem to be missing here.

441-42: These lines are rejected by many scholars as an interpolation.

478: The manuscripts contain a line here that is rejected by almost all scholars as an interpolation: "How terrible not to know the future!"

491: Text uncertain.

536-37: Many scholars reject both lines, or only the second one, as an interpolation.

545: This line is very similar to line 608 and is rejected here by many scholars.

554-56: These lines are rejected by some scholars as an interpolation.

561: This line is rejected by some scholars.

588-90: These lines too are rejected by many scholars.

593: This line is rejected by some scholars.

602-4: These lines are rejected by many scholars as an interpolation.

625: This line is identical to line 536 and is rejected here as an interpolation by many scholars.

686: This line is rejected by most scholars as an interpolation.

694-95: The second of these lines, or both of them, are rejected by most scholars.

702-3: These lines are rejected by many scholars.

714-15: Text uncertain.

847-48: The second of these lines, or both of them, are rejected by most scholars as an interpolation.

852: This line too is rejected by many scholars.

895-97: These lines are rejected by some scholars as an interpolation.

906: After this line the manuscripts transmit seven lines (907-13): "For whenever someone who is pleasing in his words / but is ill intentioned persuades the multitude, / this is a great evil for the city. But all those / who always give useful counsel with intelligence / are advantageous to the city, if not at once then later. / One should look to a leader like this: the same thing is the case / for the man who delivers speeches as for the man who holds office." These lines are rejected by most scholars as an interpolation. Lines 904-6 are also rejected by some scholars.

915: After this line the manuscripts transmit one line (916): "to the man killing you two, to speak like this." This line is rejected by most scholars.

932: After this line the manuscripts transmit one line (933): "formerly

Pelasgians, later Danaids." This line is rejected by most scholars as an interpolation.

938–42: These lines are rejected by some scholars as an interpolation.

957–59: According to ancient scholars, these three lines were missing in some manuscripts; they are rejected by many modern scholars.

960–1012: Most manuscripts assign this whole ode to Electra; most modern scholars give lines 960–81 to the chorus and 982–1012 to Electra.

982: See note on lines 960–1012.

997: Text uncertain.

1000: Text uncertain.

1006: Text uncertain.

1024: To judge from the comments of ancient scholars, this line seems to have been missing in ancient manuscripts; it is rejected by many modern scholars.

1049–51: These lines too are rejected by some scholars as an interpolation.

1106: Text uncertain.

1196: This line is rejected by many scholars as an interpolation.

1219: This line is rejected by most scholars.

1224: This line is rejected by some scholars.

1227–30: According to ancient scholars, these four lines were missing in at least one manuscript; they are rejected by many modern scholars as an interpolation.

1245: This line is rejected by many scholars.

1248–1310: Different scholars assign the lines in this section differently to the various singers and speakers.

1347–48: The manuscripts assign these lines to Orestes; modern scholars assign them to Electra instead.

1383: After this line the manuscripts transmit one line (1384): "the chariot-, chariot-song." At least some ancient scholars seem to have expressed doubts about this line, and it is rejected by most modern scholars.

1394: According to ancient scholars, this line was missing in many manuscripts; it is rejected by most modern scholars as an interpolation.

1446: Text uncertain.

1467: Text uncertain.

1484: Text uncertain.

1493: Text uncertain.

1537-48: Some manuscripts, and some modern scholars, assign some parts of this ode to the whole chorus and some parts to two half-choruses.

1564-66: These lines are rejected by some scholars as an interpolation.

1587-88: These lines too are rejected by many scholars.

1598: This line is rejected by many scholars.

1608-12: These lines are transposed by some modern scholars to come after line 1599.

1631-32: These lines are rejected by some scholars as an interpolation.

1638: This line too is rejected by many scholars.

1647: This line too is rejected by many scholars.

1691-93: These lines are rejected by most scholars as an interpolation.

GLOSSARY

Achaea, Achaean, Achaeans: a region (and its people) in Greece on the
   northern coast of the Peloponnese; sometimes used to refer to all of
   Greece (and its people).
Acheron: a river of the underworld; more generally, the underworld.
Achilles: son of Peleus and Thetis; the greatest warrior of the Greeks at
   Troy.
Acte: another name for Attica, a region of east-central Greece dominated by
   Athens.
Adrastus: king of Argos; leader of the Seven against Thebes.
Aeacus: legendary king of Aegina; father of Peleus.
Aegean: the sea to the east and south of mainland Greece.
Aegyptus: son of Belus; grandson of Poseidon; legendary king of Egypt,
   forty-nine of whose fifty sons were murdered by the fifty daughters of
   his brother Danaus.
Aerope: wife of Atreus; mother of Agamemnon and Menelaus.
Aetolia, Aetolians: a mountainous area of central Greece on the northern
   coast of the Gulf of Corinth (and its inhabitants).
Agamemnon: son of Atreus; leader of the Greek army at Troy; brother of
   Menelaus; husband of Clytemnestra, killed by her and Aegisthus upon
   his return from Troy; father of Iphigenia, Electra, and Orestes.
Agenor: a Phoenician king of Tyre; son of Poseidon and Libya; father of
   Cadmus.
Ajax: son of Telamon; important Greek hero during the Trojan War; he was
   the second-best warrior among the Achaeans (after Achilles) but lost out
   to Odysseus in the competition for the arms of Achilles after the latter's
   death, and he killed himself in rage.
Alexander: another name for Paris, son of Priam and Hecuba.
Amphiaraus: seer and king of Argos; brother-in-law of Adrastus; the most
   positively portrayed of the Seven against Thebes, he was not killed but
   swallowed up alive by the earth together with his chariot.

Amphion: one of the two mythic builders of Thebes, together with his twin brother Zethus.

Antigone: daughter of Oedipus and Jocasta; sister of Ismene and of Eteocles and Polynices.

Aphrodite: goddess of sexual desire.

Apollo: son of Zeus and Leto; twin brother of Artemis; god of prophecy, healing, roadways, music, and poetry; his prophetic seat was at Delphi.

Arcadia, Arcadian: a region (and its inhabitants) in southern Greece in the central and eastern part of the Peloponnese.

Ares: god of war.

Argive, Argives: referring to the inhabitants of Argos; sometimes used to refer in general to all the Greeks.

Argos: a city and region in the eastern Peloponnese in southern Greece, not always distinguished clearly from Mycenae.

Artemis: daughter of Zeus and Leto; twin sister of Apollo; goddess of the hunt, childbirth, and virginity, who protected wild animals and boys and girls before they reached adolescence; sometimes identified with Hecate.

Atalanta: a legendary huntress, mother of Parthenopaeus (one of the Seven against Thebes).

Athena: daughter of Zeus and Metis; goddess of wisdom, warfare, and weaving; patron goddess of Athens.

Athens: an important city in the region of Attica in the east-central part of Greece, named after Athena and protected by her; home of Greek tragedy.

Atreus: father of Agamemnon and Menelaus; brother of Thyestes.

Attic: referring to the region of Attica in the east-central part of Greece dominated by and belonging to Athens.

Avengers: the Furies (in Greek, *Erinyes*), monstrous female divinities of vengeance, who punished especially murder within the family.

Azanians: inhabitants of an area in Arcadia in southern Greece in the central and eastern part of the Peloponnese.

Bacchant: ecstatic female worshipper of Dionysus.

Bacchus, Bacchic: another name for Dionysus.

Bromius: another name for Dionysus.

Cadmean: referring to Cadmus, mythical founder of the Greek city of Thebes; more generally, Theban.

Cadmus: a Phoenician prince, son of Agenor; mythical founder of the Greek city of Thebes; he killed a dragon that protected the Castalian spring, and then, at Athena's instructions, sowed its teeth in the ground; from these sprang up armed warriors (the "Sown Men") who killed one another until only a few were left to help him found the city.

Calchas: the most important seer of the Greek army during the Trojan War.

Callisto: a nymph of Artemis who was seduced by Zeus and punished by being transformed into a bear; later she became a constellation.

Capaneus: husband of Evadne; one of the Seven against Thebes; he boasted that he would sack the city whether Zeus wished it or not, and while he was mounting a ladder to attack the walls Zeus killed him with a thunderbolt.

Cape Malea: the most southeasterly peninsula of the Peloponnese in southern Greece.

Caphereus: a promontory on the southeast coast of Euboea on which Nauplius set up deceptive fire signals to mislead and destroy the Greek fleet as it returned from Troy.

Castalia: a fountain at Delphi at the foot of Mount Parnassus.

Castor: together with Polydeuces (or Pollux), one of the twin sons of Tyndareus; brother of Helen and Clytemnestra; a divinity who protected mariners in distress.

Cecrops: a legendary king of Athens.

Chrysothemis: a third daughter of Agamemnon and Clytemnestra; sister of Iphigenia, Orestes, and Electra.

Cithaeron: a mountain in central Greece near Thebes.

Clytemnestra: wife of Agamemnon; together with her lover Aegisthus she killed her husband on his return from Troy; mother of Iphigenia, Electra, and Orestes; she was killed in revenge by Orestes and Electra. Also written Clytaemestra.

Colonus: a district in Attica to the northwest of Athens where Oedipus was buried.

Creon: son of Menoeceus; brother of Jocasta; father of Menoeceus; king of Thebes after the destitution of Oedipus and the deaths of Eteocles and Polynices.

Crete: an important Greek island to the southeast of mainland Greece.

Cyclopean: referring to the massive walls of Mycenae and other cities, built by the Cyclopes according to legend.

Cypris: Aphrodite; according to some accounts she was born in the Mediterranean Sea near Cyprus and came first to land on that island; she was worshipped in an especially strong cult there.

Cyprus: an important Greek and Phoenician island in the southeast Mediterranean off the south coast of Anatolia (modern-day Turkey).

Danaans: descendants of Danaus, a hero who was one of the legendary founders of Argos; in general, Argives and, more generally, all the Greeks.

Danaid: referring to the descendants of Danaus; in general, Argives and, more generally, all the Greeks. Alternatively, referring to the fifty daughters of Danaus, forty-nine of whom killed on their wedding night the cousins they were obliged to marry.

Danaus: brother of Aegyptus; a hero who was one of the legendary founders of Argos.

Dardanus, Dardanians: the Trojans, said to be the descendants of Dardanus, one of the city's legendary founders.

Delphi: the major oracle and cult center of Apollo, situated on Mount Parnassus in central Greece.

Demeter: goddess of fertility, mother of Persephone (Kore); when Persephone was abducted by Hades, Demeter searched for her with such singleminded grief that she stopped the change of seasons and organic growth until Zeus arranged for Persephone to be restored to her for at least part of the year.

Deo: another name for Demeter, goddess of fertility, mother of Persephone.

Diomedes: legendary Greek hero, king of Argos; a leading warrior during the Trojan War.

Dione: Greek goddess, mother of Aphrodite according to some accounts.

Dioscuri: Castor and Polydeuces (Pollux), the twin brothers of Helen and Clytemnestra; divinities who protected mariners in distress.

Dirce: a fountain and river in Thebes.

Dodona: an oracle of Zeus in Epirus in northwestern Greece.

Egypt: a region and country in North Africa, on the southeastern coast of the Mediterranean.

Eido: the name given to Theonoë when she was a child; it may mean "Beauty" or perhaps "Knowing."

Electra: daughter of Agamemnon and Clytemnestra; sister of Iphigenia and Orestes.

Electran gate: one of the seven city gates of Thebes, leading out toward Cithaeron.

Epaphus: son of Zeus and Io; legendary ancestor of both the Argives and the Tyrians.

Erechtheus: a legendary king of Athens.

Eteocles: son of Oedipus and Jocasta; brother of Antigone and Ismene and of Polynices; his name means "True Fame."

Euboea, Euboean: a large island off the coast of eastern mainland Greece, north of Athens.

Eumenides: monstrous female divinities of vengeance who punished especially murder within the family; also called Furies; "Eumenides" is euphemistic and means "Well-Wishers."

Eumolpus: legendary king of Thrace who attacked Athens.

Eurotas: a river near Sparta in the Peloponnese.

Fury, Furies: monstrous female divinities of vengeance who punished especially murder within the family; in Greek "Erinyes," but also euphemistically called Eumenides.

Galaneia: a sea divinity responsible for calm seas without winds.

Gate of Proetus: one of the seven gates of the city of Thebes.

Gate of Springs: one of the seven gates of the city of Thebes.

Geraestus: site of a temple of Poseidon in the southern part of the island of Euboea facing the Myrtoan Sea, said to have been named after Myrtilus.

Giant: one of the children of Earth, sometimes identified with the Titans, who fought against the Olympian gods and were defeated by them.

Glaucus: a divinity of the sea who assisted mariners with prophecy and advice.

Gorgon: Medusa, one of three monstrous snake-women whose face was so terrifying that whoever looked on it was turned to stone; killed by Perseus.

Graces: companions of Aphrodite; goddesses of all kinds of beauty and charm.

Great Mother: another name for the Mountain Mother, Cybele; occasionally identified with Demeter (Deo.)

Hades: brother of Zeus and Poseidon; god of the underworld; his name is used synonymously for the underworld itself.

Haemon: son of Creon, promised in marriage to Antigone.

Harmonia: daughter of Aphrodite; wife of Cadmus; mother of Polydorus.

Hebe: the goddess of youth, married to Heracles after his death and apotheosis.

Hecate: goddess associated with witchcraft, night, doorways, crossroads, and the moon; sometimes identified with Artemis.

Helen: daughter of Leda and either Zeus or Tyndareus; wife of Menelaus (the brother of Agamemnon) and mother of Hermione; her (putative) elopement with Paris caused the Trojan War.

Helenus: a son of Priam; a seer for the Trojans.

Hellas, Hellene, Hellenes, Hellenic: Greece, Greek, the Greeks.

Hera: wife and sister of Zeus; queen of the gods; goddess of marriage; she had an important cult center at Argos; the exact location on Cithaeron of "Hera's Field" is unknown.

Heracles: son of Zeus and Alcmene; the greatest hero of Greek legend.

Hermes: son of Zeus and Maia; the messenger god; god of travelers, contests, stealth, and heralds, who escorted the souls of the dead to the underworld.

Hermione: daughter of Menelaus and Helen.

Hippomedon: one of the Seven against Thebes.

Homoloid gate: one of the seven gates of the city of Thebes.

Hyacinthus: a beautiful boy beloved by Apollo, who accidentally killed him by hitting him with a discus he threw.

Hydra: mythical monster with many heads that grew back whenever one was cut off; killed by Heracles.

Ida, Idaean: a mountain near Troy, where Paris judged a beauty contest between Hera, Athena, and Aphrodite; Paris assigned the victory to Aphrodite, who rewarded him with Helen.

Ilium: Troy.

Inachus: the main river of Argos; in mythology, Inachus was the father of Io, who bore to Zeus Epaphus, the ancestor of the royal house of Argos.

Io: daughter of Inachus; she bore Epaphus to Zeus; because of Hera's jealousy, Io was transformed into a heifer and tormented by a gadfly.

Ionians: one of the four major tribes of ancient Greece; the Ionian Sea lies to the west of mainland Greece and southeast of Italy.

Iphigenia: daughter of Agamemnon and Clytemnestra; when adverse winds blocked the Greek fleet at Aulis from sailing to Troy, Agamemnon had her brought there and was thought to have sacrificed her to Artemis (but in some versions Artemis spirited her away and put a deer in her place).

Island of the Blest: a legendary, utopian island where a few heroes enjoyed a blissful life after death.

Ismene: daughter of Oedipus and Jocasta; sister of Antigone and of Eteocles and Polynices.

Ismenus: a river in Boeotia that flows through Thebes.

Jocasta: wife of Laius; mother and wife of Oedipus; mother of Antigone and Ismene and of Eteocles and Polynices; sister of Creon.

Kore: Persephone, daughter of Demeter; abducted by Hades.

Labdacus: son of Polydorus; father of Laius; founder of the Labdacids, the ruling dynasty of Thebes, including Laius, his son Oedipus, and his sons Eteocles and Polynices.

Lacedaemon: Sparta.

Laconian: referring to Laconia, a region in southern Greece in the southeastern part of the Peloponnese; Sparta is situated there.

Laius: king of Thebes; husband of Jocasta; an oracle warned him not to beget a child; when he disobeyed and Jocasta bore a son, he had him exposed on Cithaeron; but the baby was rescued and grew up to become Oedipus, and eventually killed Laius.

Leda: mythical queen of Sparta; wife of Tyndareus; seduced by Zeus who visited her in the form of a swan; the mother of Castor and Polydeuces and of Helen and Clytemnestra.

Lerna: a marshy area south of Argos near the eastern coast of the Peloponnese in southern Greece; home of the Hydra.

Leto: goddess, the mother of Apollo and Artemis.

Leucippus: father of two daughters, Hilaeira and Phoebe, who were venerated in a cult in Sparta.

Libya, Libyan: a region in North Africa on the southern coast of the Mediterranean.

Lord of Gold and Death: Plutus, god of wealth, sometimes associated or identified with Hades/Pluto, the god of the underworld.

Loxias: Apollo; the word means "slanting" and may refer to the ambiguity of his oracles.

maenads: ecstatic female worshippers of Dionysus.

Maia: a nymph, who bore Hermes to Zeus.

Menelaus: brother of Agamemnon; husband of Helen; father of Hermione.

Menoeceus: (1) father of Creon and Jocasta; (2) son of Creon.

Merops: father of Cos, a nymph of Artemis who was banished from her retinue and transformed into a deer.

Mountain Mother: another name for the Great Mother, Cybele; occasionally identified with Demeter (Deo).

Muses: daughters of Mnemosyne and Zeus, associated with all forms of cultural excellence, especially artistic, musical, and poetic.

Mycenae, Mycenaeans: an ancient city (and its inhabitants) in Greece in the northeastern Peloponnese, not always distinguished clearly from nearby Argos.

Myrtilus: charioteer of Oenomaus, the father of Hippodamea. Oenomaus challenged all suitors of her hand to a chariot race and killed them when they lost; eventually Pelops bribed Myrtilus, who sabotaged Oenomaus' chariot so that he was killed during the race. Pelops then killed Myrtilus.

Naiad: a nymph associated with fountains and streams.

Nauplia: a harbor on the eastern coast of the Peloponnese (modern-day Nafplion).

Nauplius: father of Palamedes, in revenge for whose death at the hands of his fellow Greeks he set up deceptive fire-signals on the coast of Euboea at Caphereus in order to mislead and destroy the Greek fleet as it returned from Troy.

Neïstan gates: one of the seven gates of the city of Thebes.

Nemesis: goddess of vengeance.

Neoptolemus: son of Achilles; notorious for his brutality at the sack of Troy (he killed Priam at an altar); afterward he took Andromache as slave and concubine, and was later killed at Delphi; also known as Pyrrhus.

Nereids: fifty sea nymphs, daughters of Nereus.

Nereus: a divinity of the sea; father of the fifty Nereids; famous for his wisdom.

Nestor: aged warrior and counselor of the Greek army during the Trojan War; his son Antilochus famously died to save his father's life.

New Salamis: Greek city in Cyprus founded as a colony by inhabitants of the island Salamis near Athens.

Nile: the most important river of Egypt, famous for its annual floods.

Niobe: a Greek heroine; when she boasted that she had many children, while Leto had only two, Apollo and Artemis, these latter were offended and killed all of her children with their arrows.

Odysseus: Greek warrior at Troy, famous for his cleverness; husband of Penelope.

Oeax: son of Nauplius and brother of Palamedes.

Oedipus: son of Laius and Jocasta, exposed at birth with pins thrust through his ankles (his name means "Swollen-foot"); he was rescued and grew up to kill his father, solve the riddle of the Sphinx, marry his mother, and beget with her four children, Antigone and Ismene, and Eteocles and Polynices; when he found out, he blinded himself in horror at what he had done.

Oeneus: legendary Greek king, father of Tydeus.

Oenomaus: father of Hippodamea. He challenged all suitors of her hand to a chariot race and killed them when they lost; eventually Pelops bribed Oenomaus' charioteer Myrtilus, who sabotaged Oenomaus' chariot so that he was killed during the race.

Ogygian gate: one of the seven gates of the city of Thebes.

Olympus: a mountain on which the gods make their home, located in Pieria in northern Greece.

Oresteion: a town in Parrhasia in southern Arcadia, thought to have been founded by Orestes.

Orestes: son of Agamemnon and Clytemnestra; brother of Iphigenia and Electra; he killed his mother to avenge his father.

Orion: a legendary gigantic hunter, placed after his death among the stars.

paean: a kind of poem addressed to Apollo and imploring or celebrating his help.

Palamedes: Greek warrior at Troy, treacherously killed by the Greeks through the machinations of Odysseus. In revenge, his father Nauplius sabotaged the Greek fleet as it returned from Troy.

Pallas: Athena.

Pan: a rustic, musical god dwelling in wild nature and associated with sudden mental disturbances (hence our term "panic").

Paris: son of Priam and Hecuba; his elopement with Helen caused the Trojan War; also known as Alexander.

Parnassus: a mountain above Delphi in central Greece, associated with Apollo and the Muses.

Parrhasia: a region of southern Arcadia in southern Greece in the central and eastern part of the Peloponnese.

Parthenopaeus: son of Atalanta; one of the Seven against Thebes.

Pelasgia: a vague geographical term that may refer to Arcadia, the Peloponnese, or all of Greece.

Peleus: father of Achilles.

Pelopidae: the royal dynasty of Argos/Mycenae, descended from Pelops.

Pelops: son of Tantalus; a mythical king of the city of Pisa; the Peloponnese in southern Greece is named after him.

Periclymenus: son of Poseidon; one of the Theban defenders against the attack of the Seven against Thebes.

Persephone: daughter of Demeter; wife of Hades and queen of the underworld; also called Kore.

Perseus' watchtower: a landmark of unknown location, perhaps on the farthest western shore of the Mediterranean.

Pharos: an island off the coast of the Nile Delta in Egypt, home of Proteus.

Phocis: a region in central Greece on the northern shore of the Gulf of Corinth.

Phoebus: epithet of Apollo meaning "bright."

Phoenicia, Phoenician: a country (and its people) in the Levant on the eastern coast of the Mediterranean, including the cities of Tyre and Sidon; famous for naval and commercial activity.

Phrygian, Phrygians: referring to inhabitants of Phrygia, a kingdom in what is now west-central Turkey; often used as a synonym for the Trojans.

Pisan: referring to Pisa, a city in the Peloponnese in southern Greece once ruled by the legendary Pelops.

Pleiades: nymphs, daughters of Atlas, who were turned into a cluster of stars.

Polybus: legendary king of Corinth; when Oedipus was exposed as a baby on Cithaeron, he was taken up by one of Polybus' shepherds, who brought him to the king; Polybus adopted him and raised him as his own.

Polydeuces: together with Castor, one of the twin sons of Tyndareus; brother of Helen and Clytemnestra; a divinity who protected mariners in distress; also known as Pollux.

Polydorus: son of Cadmus and Harmonia; father of Labdacus.

Polynices: son of Oedipus and Jocasta; brother of Antigone and Ismene and of Eteocles; his name means "Much Strife."

Poseidon: brother of Zeus; god of the sea, of horses, and of earthquakes.

Potniae: hometown of Glaucus, who fed his mares on human flesh.

Priam: king of Troy; husband of Hecuba; father of Paris, Hector, Cassandra, and many other sons and daughters; killed by Achilles' son Neoptolemus at the altar of Zeus during the fall of Troy.

Prometheus: one of the Titans; he stole fire in a fennel stalk and gave it to humankind.

Proteus: originally a sea god, identified with a mythical Egyptian king celebrated for his wisdom; according to some versions, the real Helen stayed with him while an image of her was brought to Troy by Paris and was fought over during the Trojan War.

Psamathe: wife first of Aeacus, then of Proteus, to whom she bore Theoclymenus and Theonoë.

Pylades: son of Strophius of Phocis; the loyal comrade of Orestes.

Pythian: belonging to Delphi (where Apollo had killed the giant snake Python).

Salamis: an island near Athens.

Scamander: a river near Troy.

Selene: goddess of the moon.

Semele: a Theban princess, daughter of Cadmus; mother of Dionysus by Zeus.

Sicily: an island to the southwest of Italy.

Sidon: one of the most important Phoenician cities, on the eastern coast of the Mediterranean, famous for the naval and commercial activity of its inhabitants.

Sidonian: referring to Sidon.

Simois: a river near Troy.

Sirens: mythical female singers whose song was fatally seductive.

Sown Men: according to Theban legend, the original inhabitants of the city, who sprang from the ground, from the teeth of a dragon that Cadmus sowed; in Greek, *Spartoi*.

Sparta: an important city in the southeastern Peloponnese in southern Greece.

Sphinx: a monstrous and deadly mythical figure, part woman, part animal; she infested Thebes and killed its youth as long as a riddle she posed could not be answered; when Oedipus answered it, she died.

Strophius: king of Phocis; father of Pylades; when Clytemnestra and Aegisthus killed Agamemnon, Orestes was rescued and brought to Strophius for safekeeping.

Talthybius: a herald of the Greek army at Troy.

Tantalus: father of Pelops; founder of the house of Atreus to which
Agamemnon and Menelaus belonged.

Teiresias: blind seer of Thebes.

Telamon, Telamonian: Greek hero, father of Ajax and Teucer.

Telemachus: son of Odysseus and Penelope.

Teucer: son of Telamon; half-brother of Ajax and his comrade during the
Trojan War.

Teumessus: ancient town in Boeotia near Thebes.

Thebes, Theban: a large city (and its inhabitants) in the southern part of the
region of Boeotia in central Greece.

Theoclymenus: king of Egypt; son of Proteus and Psamathe; brother of
Theonoë; his name means "God-renowned" or "God-inspired."

Theonoë: daughter of Proteus and Psamathe; sister of Theoclymenus; her
name means "God-mind, she who knows godly matters."

Thesprotia: a region, part of Epirus, on the northwestern coast of Greece.

Thessaly, Thessalian: a large region (and its people) in the north-central
part of Greece.

Thestius: father of Leda.

Thetis: sea nymph, one of the fifty daughters of Nereus; wife of Peleus and
mother of Achilles.

Thyestes: brother of Atreus, bound to him by a furious hatred; father of
Aegisthus.

thyrsus: a wand carried by worshippers of Dionysus, made of a fennel stalk
with ivy vines and leaves wound around its tip and topped by a pine
cone.

Titanian: referring to the Titans, primeval divinities defeated by Zeus,
Athena, and the other Olympian gods.

Troy: city in northwestern Anatolia (now northwestern Turkey), defeated
and pillaged by a Greek army; also known as Ilium.

Tydeus: one of the Seven against Thebes; father of Diomedes.

Tyndareus: king of Sparta; husband of Leda, father of Castor and Polydeuces
and of Helen and Clytemnestra.

Tyre, Tyrian: an ancient Phoenician city, original home of Cadmus.

Tyrrhenian: Etruscan; the war trumpet was thought to have been an Etruscan invention.

Zethus: one of the two mythical builders of Thebes, together with his twin
brother Amphion.

Zeus: king of gods and men.